SMITH WIGGLESWORTH on FAITH

Other Titles
by Smith Wigglesworth

Ever Increasing Faith

Experiencing God's Power Today

Greater Works

The Power of Faith

Smith Wigglesworth Devotional

*Smith Wigglesworth: The Complete Collection
of His Life Teachings*
(compiled by Roberts Liardon)

Smith Wigglesworth on Healing

Smith Wigglesworth on Heaven

Smith Wigglesworth Only Believe

Smith Wigglesworth on Spirit-Filled Living

Smith Wigglesworth on Spiritual Gifts

Smith Wigglesworth on the Holy Spirit

Smith Wigglesworth on the Power of Scripture
(compiled by Roberts Liardon)

*Smith Wigglesworth: The Complete Collection
of His Life Teachings*
(compiled by Roberts Liardon)

Wigglesworth on the Anointing

SMITH WIGGLESWORTH on FAITH

SMITH WIGGLESWORTH

WHITAKER
HOUSE

Whitaker House gratefully acknowledges and thanks Glenn Gohr and the entire staff of the Assemblies of God Archives in Springfield, Missouri, for graciously assisting us in compiling Smith Wigglesworth's works for publication in this book.

Unless otherwise indicated, all Scripture quotations are taken from the *New King James Version* (NKJV), © 1979, 1980, 1982, 1984 by Thomas Nelson, Inc. Used by permission. All rights reserved.
All Scripture quotations marked (KJV) are taken from the King James Version of the Holy Bible.

Publisher's note: This new edition from Whitaker House has been updated for the modern reader. Words, expressions, and sentence structure have been revised for clarity and readability. Although the more modern Bible translation quoted in this edition was not available to Smith Wigglesworth, it was carefully and prayerfully selected in order to make the language of the entire text readily understandable while maintaining his original premises and message.

SMITH WIGGLESWORTH ON FAITH

ISBN-13: 978-0-88368-531-0 • ISBN-10: 0-88368-531-0
Printed in the United States of America
© 1998 by Whitaker House

Whitaker House
1030 Hunt Valley Circle
New Kensington, PA 15068
www.whitakerhouse.com

Library of Congress Cataloging-in-Publication Data

Wigglesworth, Smith, 1859–1947.
    Smith Wigglesworth on faith / by Smith Wigglesworth.
        p.   cm.
    ISBN 0-88368-531-0 (trade paper)
    1. Faith. 2. Pentecostal churches—Doctrines. I. Title.
BT771.2.W54 1998
234'.23—dc21
                                          98-17884

9 10 11 12 13 14 15 ␣␣ 16 15 14 13 12 11 10

Contents

Introduction...7

1. The Author and Finisher of Our Faith.................13

2. Dominant Faith...19

3. Faith Based upon Knowledge............................25

4. Faith Is the Victory..................................33

5. The Faith of God.......................................43

6. Faith's Treasures.....................................59

7. The Inheritance of Faith..............................79

8. Full! Full! Full!.....................................93

9. Have Faith in God....................................103

10. The Hour Is Come.....................................113

11. Filled with God's Fullness...........................123

12. A Living Faith..127

13. The Blessed Reality of God...........................135

14. The Substance of Things Hoped For...................141

15. The Way of Faith.....................................153

16. The Way to Overcome..................................165

17. Only Believe...169

18. By Faith...189

19. Like Precious Faith..................................197

Introduction

An encounter with Smith Wigglesworth was an unforgettable experience. This seems to be the universal reaction of all who knew him or heard him speak. Smith Wigglesworth was a simple yet remarkable man who was used in an extraordinary way by our extraordinary God. He had a contagious and inspiring faith. Under his ministry, thousands of people came to salvation, committed themselves to a deeper faith in Christ, received the baptism in the Holy Spirit, and were miraculously healed. The power that brought these kinds of results was the presence of the Holy Spirit, who filled Smith Wigglesworth and used him in bringing the good news of the Gospel to people all over the world. Wigglesworth gave glory to God for everything that was accomplished through his ministry, and he wanted people to understand his work only in this context, because his sole desire was that people would see Jesus and not himself.

Smith Wigglesworth was born in England in 1859. Immediately after his conversion as a boy, he had a concern for the salvation of others and won people to Christ, including his mother. Even so, as a young man, he could not express himself well enough to give a testimony in church, much less preach a sermon. Wigglesworth said that his mother had the same difficulty in expressing herself that he did. This family trait, coupled with the fact that he

7

had no formal education because he began working twelve hours a day at the age of seven to help support the family, contributed to Wigglesworth's awkward speaking style. He became a plumber by trade, yet he continued to devote himself to winning many people to Christ on an individual basis.

In 1882, he married Polly Featherstone, a vivacious young woman who loved God and had a gift of preaching and evangelism. It was she who taught him to read and who became his closest confidant and strongest supporter. They both had compassion for the poor and needy in their community, and they opened a mission, at which Polly preached. Significantly, people were miraculously healed when Wigglesworth prayed for them.

In 1907, Wigglesworth's circumstances changed dramatically when, at the age of forty-eight, he was baptized in the Holy Spirit. Suddenly, he had a new power that enabled him to preach, and even his wife was amazed at the transformation. This was the beginning of what became a worldwide evangelistic and healing ministry that reached thousands. He eventually ministered in the United States, Australia, South Africa, and all over Europe. His ministry extended up to the time of his death in 1947.

Several emphases in Smith Wigglesworth's life and ministry characterize him: a genuine, deep compassion for the unsaved and sick; an unflinching belief in the Word of God; a desire that Christ should increase and he should decrease (John 3:30); a belief that he was called to exhort people to enlarge their faith and trust in God; an emphasis on the baptism in the Holy Spirit with the manifestation of the gifts of the Spirit as in the early church;

and a belief in complete healing for everyone of all sickness.

Smith Wigglesworth was called "The Apostle of Faith" because absolute trust in God was a constant theme of both his life and his messages. In his meetings, he would quote passages from the Word of God and lead lively singing to help build people's faith and encourage them to act on it. He emphasized belief in the fact that God could do the impossible. He had great faith in what God could do, and God did great things through him.

Wigglesworth's unorthodox methods were often questioned. As a person, Wigglesworth was reportedly courteous, kind, and gentle. However, he became forceful when dealing with the devil, whom he believed caused all sickness. Wigglesworth said the reason he spoke bluntly and acted forcefully with people was that he knew he needed to get their attention so they could focus on God. He also had such anger toward the devil and sickness that he acted in a seemingly rough way. When he prayed for people to be healed, he would often hit or punch them at the place of their problem or illness. Yet, no one was hurt by this startling treatment. Instead, they were remarkably healed. When he was asked why he treated people in this manner, he said that he was not hitting the people but that he was hitting the devil. He believed that Satan should never be treated gently or allowed to get away with anything. About twenty people were reportedly raised from the dead after he prayed for them. Wigglesworth himself was healed of appendicitis and kidney stones, after which his personality softened and he was more gentle with those who came to him for prayer for healing. His abrupt manner in ministering may be attributed to the fact that he was very serious about his calling and got down to business quickly.

Although Wigglesworth believed in complete healing, he encountered illnesses and deaths that were difficult to understand. These included the deaths of his wife and son, his daughter's lifelong deafness, and his own battles with kidney stones and sciatica.

He often seemed paradoxical: compassionate but forceful, blunt but gentle, a well-dressed gentleman whose speech was often ungrammatical or confusing. However, he loved God with everything he had, he was steadfastly committed to God and to His Word, and he didn't rest until he saw God move in the lives of those who needed Him.

In 1936, Smith Wigglesworth prophesied about what we now know as the charismatic movement. He accurately predicted that the established mainline denominations would experience revival and the gifts of the Spirit in a way that would surpass even the Pentecostal movement. Wigglesworth did not live to see the renewal, but as an evangelist and prophet with a remarkable healing ministry, he had a tremendous influence on both the Pentecostal and charismatic movements, and his example and influence on believers is felt to this day.

Without the power of God that was so obviously present in his life and ministry, we might not be reading transcripts of his sermons, for his spoken messages were often disjointed and ungrammatical. However, true gems of spiritual insight shine through them because of the revelation he received through the Holy Spirit. It was his life of complete devotion and belief in God and his reliance on the Holy Spirit that brought the life-changing power of God into his messages.

As you read this book, it is important to remember that Wigglesworth's works span a period of several decades, from the early 1900s to the 1940s. They were originally presented as spoken rather than written messages, and necessarily retain some of the flavor of a church service or prayer meeting. At his meetings, he would often speak in tongues and give the interpretation, and these messages have been included as well. Because of Wigglesworth's unique style, the sermons in this book have been edited for clarity, and archaic expressions that would be unfamiliar to modern readers have been updated.

In conclusion, we hope that as you read these words of Smith Wigglesworth, you will truly sense his complete trust and unwavering faith in God and take to heart one of his favorite sayings: "Only believe!"

1

The Author and Finisher of Our Faith

P raise the Lord that I have had the opportunity to spend over a month in Canaan. I have crossed the river of Jordan; been on the lake of Galilee; bathed in the Dead Sea; drunk at Jacob's well; had a drink at Elijah's fountain; preached on the top of the Mount of Olives; stood with tears running down my face just opposite Mount Calvary, and with hands lifted up, seen the place of sacrifice; and passed by the spot where the holy inn stood in Bethlehem. As I thought of all the holy associations connected with that land, my heart was melted. God has been very good to me.

Glorious Jesus

One of my favorite texts is in the twelfth chapter of Hebrews. I want to look at a few verses there. What a wonderful revelation Hebrews is to us.

Therefore we also, since we are surrounded by so great a cloud of witnesses, let us lay aside

every weight, and the sin which so easily en-
snares us, and let us run with endurance the
race that is set before us, looking unto Jesus, the
author and finisher of our faith.   (Heb. 12:1–2)

The thought here is Jesus as the Author and
Finisher of our faith. Glory to God. What a sight to
see our Lord Jesus Christ come forth robed in His
own majesty and glory, as no man was ever robed.
He is clothed in majesty. What compassion He had
when He saw the struggling multitude! When He
saw the crowds in need, His heart yearned with
compassion. How He handled the bread! (See Matthew 14:15–21; 15:32–38.) No man ever handled
bread like Jesus did. I can almost look into His face
and see His eyes glisten as He sees the multitude. He
said to Philip, "I would like to feed these people; how
much would it take to feed them?" Philip said,
"Eight months' wages is not sufficient, and besides,
this is a desert place." (See Mark 6:37.)

If you have been to Palestine and seen the sights
I have seen, you understand what is meant by a desert place. I looked for many things in the Scriptures
while I was over there, and God has spoken to me
through the experience. They have the early and the
latter rain there, and the land is a beautiful land.
Praise the Lord!

It was lovely to be there and see these things,
but, beloved, it made me cherish the Bible as I have
never cherished it before. Why? Because God has
given us the assurance that makes our hearts know
it is true. Even if you never see the Holy Land, you
can live in the Holy Land and see all the wonderful
things and read of them in your Bible.

The Author and Finisher of Our Faith

Beloved, I want to speak on the Author and the Finisher of our faith, and I want us to remember that Abraham, Daniel, and all the prophets were men of faith. We must not look at the things that have been done in the past; we must look at Jesus, the Author and the Finisher of our faith. We must *"run with endurance the race that is set before us, looking unto Jesus"* (Heb. 12:1–2). We must so look at the Author and the Finisher of our faith that the same glory and power will be resting upon us as was upon Him. We must have such grace, such holiness, that we will be landmarks showing His power is upon us.

Praise the Lord. Don't stumble at what I am going to say, but praise God that we not only have the abiding presence of the Spirit's power in our midst, but we have the living Word, the living Christ. He is the Author and the Finisher of our faith. He has given eternal life to us, that is, if we have His Word and believe.

My dear wife has now entered glory, but during her lifetime she was a great revivalist. She was a preacher. I have seen the mighty power of God fall upon her and have seen her face light up with a heavenly light as she preached, and there are many ministers of the Gospel today because of her preaching and her faithfulness, and others are missionaries and working for God. We will never know the extent of her work until the last day. You see, beloved, as we are faithful to God and come into line with Him and labor for Him, our work will be rewarded. A great crowd is looking on. God is doing a work in these days, and these are days of opportunity.

Faith Is Working Now

God has been blessing New Zealand, and you must hear all about that land. In Australia, four hundred people were baptized in the Holy Spirit. The Holy Spirit is being poured out everywhere, and the tide of blessing is rising. The power of the Holy Spirit is greater than we have ever conceived. The basis of the Pentecostal testimony should be holiness. What is the strength of our position today? Holiness. I say to you, if you fall a thousand times in a week, strive to be holy. It does not matter how many times you fall; do not give in because you fall.

I was staying in a house, and the lady of the house prepared a room and a bed for me to rest on, because I had just gotten off the train and was very tired. When I awoke she said, "I want you to lie in my son's bed. I would like him to know you have lain in the bed." I slept in that bed for three nights, and later two people slept in the same bed and both got baptized in the Spirit. Hallelujah! I desire that every person who is seeking would get baptized.

That lady had such a sense of the presence of God that she said, "Lie in my son's bed." As soon as I opened my eyes, I looked across the room and saw these words: "A man does not fall because he makes a blunder, he falls because he makes a blunder the second time." God does not want us to fall but to be kept by His grace from falling, and He wants us to strive for holiness. I see the Word of God is the living Word, and Jesus is the Author of the Word. The Holy Spirit is the enlightener of the Word. If you look at Acts 1, you will see these words: *"He through the Holy Spirit had given commandments"* (v. 2).

16

We will find as we go on that the Lord Jesus Christ is the Author of our lives. He is the source of our life, our spiritual life, and He is producing holiness.

I want you to see what David said in the sixty-third Psalm: *"So I have looked for You in the sanctuary, to see Your power and Your glory,"* (v. 2). Jesus said, *"Father, glorify Me together with Yourself, with the glory which I had with You before the world was"* (John 17:5). The greatest glory that was ever seen was manifested on the cross. The glory was manifested when Jesus offered Himself, *"through the eternal Spirit"* (Heb. 9:14), on the cross. He said to Judas, *"What you do, do quickly....Now the Son of Man is glorified"* (John 13:27, 31). So we see that God was glorified in Jesus; He was reconciling the world unto Himself (2 Cor. 5:19).

Everyone who has desires for God should believe the Word of God and take Jesus as the Author and the Finisher of his faith. All the desires and purposes of your heart will be accomplished, because God is faithful. God cannot fail; His Word is true. But what is real Pentecost? It is the manifestation of the power of God, and it is the manifestation of the power of the Holy Spirit. Real Pentecost is the manifestation of the signs and wonders. Real Pentecost is manifested in those who are *"determined not to know anything among* [men] *except Jesus Christ and Him crucified"* (1 Cor. 2:2). I say now, as I have said before, *"Whom have I in heaven but You? And there is none upon earth that I desire besides You"* (Ps. 73:25). He is my all in all. Amen.

2

Dominant Faith

*Now faith is the substance of things hoped for, the
evidence of things not seen. For by it the elders
obtained a good testimony. By faith we understand
that the worlds were framed by the word of God, so
that the things which are seen were not made of
things which are visible.*
—Hebrews 11:1–3

aith is the substance, and it is a reality. God
wants to bring us to the fact of it. He wants
us to know that we have something greater
than we can see or handle, because everything we
can see and handle is going to pass away. The heavens are going to be wrapped up, the earth will melt
with fervent heat, but the Word of the Lord will
abide forever. *"By faith we understand that the
worlds were framed by the word of God, so that the
things which are seen were not made of things which
are visible."*

God spoke the Word and made the world, and I
want to impress upon you this wonderful Word that
made the world. I am saved by the incorruptible

Word, the Word that made the world, and so my position by faith is to lay hold of the things that cannot be seen and believe the things that cannot be understood.

Faith Lives in a Commanding Position

God will work the miracle, if you dare to stand upon the Word. Paul related his conversion many times over, and I believe it is good to rehearse what God has done for you. I have been privileged to travel to every part of the world and have seen that God has arranged a plan for me. I said to my congregation, "The Lord is moving me to go out through the States and Canada." When the Lord told me, I said, "Lord, You have three things to do: You have to find money for home and find money to go, and You have to give me a real change, for You know that sometimes my mind or memory is no good at all to me."

Right away money came from all over, and I said, "It is true God is sending me. I already have fifty pounds." My son George said, "Father, Mother's gone to heaven, and you are leaving us; what will we do?" A letter came, and I said, "George, you open the letter." And for six weeks a check had been coming for twenty-five pounds.

I went to Liverpool, and a man said, "Here is five pounds for you." When I was on the ship, a poorly-dressed lady gave me a red sugar bag, and there were twenty-five gold coins in it. Just as I was getting on the ship, a man came and gave me a book and said, "There is a page for every day in the year." And the Lord said to me, "Put down everything that takes place in the month." I did so, and I had a memory like an encyclopedia. You see, I never learned geography, and God sent me all over the world to see it.

Live in a Place of Command

The Lord has a way of making you equal to living in the power of the Holy Spirit as long as you have learned the needed lesson. God will make us know how to live.

I went to a Quakers' meeting, quiet and still, and there was such a silence that I was moved. It was of faith, and so I jumped up and had the time of my life. All these Quakers came round me, and they said, "You are the first man that we have ever seen in this place who was so quickly led by the Spirit." I said, "If the Spirit does not move me, I move the Spirit. John says it is the anointing of the Holy One (1 John 2:20), and you need no man to teach you (v. 27). It is the Holy Spirit who teaches. It is simplicity itself."

While on a ship, I said to the people, "I am going to preach on this ship on Sunday; will you come and hear me preach?"

They said no. Later they came around again and said, "We are going to have some entertainment, and we would like you to be in it."

So I said, "Come in a quarter of an hour, and I will tell you."

They came round again and said, "Are you ready?"

"Yes," I told them, "I have got a clear witness that I have to be in the entertainment."

They said, "Well, what can you do?"

I replied, "I can sing."

They said, "Now we want to know what position you would like to have on the program."

I answered, "Tell me what you are going to have on the program."

They said, "Recitations, instruments, and many things."

I asked, "What will you finish up with?"

"A dance."

"Well, put me down just before the dance."

I went to the entertainment, and when I saw the clergymen trying to please the people, it turned me to prayer. When they had all done their pieces, my turn came, and I went up to the piano with my "Redemption Songs." When the lady, who was rather less than half dressed, saw the music, she said, "I cannot play this kind of music."

I said, "Be at peace, young lady. I have music and words inside." So I sang:

If I could only tell Him as I know Him.
My Redeemer who has brightened all my way;
If I could tell how precious in His presence,
I am sure that you would make Him yours today.
Could I tell it, Could I tell it,
How the sunshine of His presence lights my way.
I would tell it, I would tell it,
And I'm sure that you would make Him yours today.

God took it up, and from the least to the greatest they were weeping. They never had a dance, but they had a prayer meeting. Six young men were saved by the power of God in my cabin.

Dominant Faith

Live in the Acts of the Apostles, and every day you will see some miracle worked by the power of the living God. It comes right to the threshold, and God brings everything along to you.

Claim Your Holy Position

Do not fail to claim your holy position, so that you will overcome the power of the devil. The best time you have is when you are in the most difficult position.

You know, sometimes it seems as though the strangest things happen for the furtherance of the Gospel. I was at Southampton station, and there were four men to see me into the train. They knew everything, and I knew nothing, only I soon found that I was in the wrong carriage. There was a man in the carriage, and I said to him, "I have been to Bournemouth before, but I do not seem to be going the right way. Where are you going?"

He said, "I am going to South Wales."

I said, "What is the Lord Jesus Christ to you? He is my personal Friend and Savior."

The man replied, "I do not thank you to speak to me about these things."

The train stopped, and I said to the porter, "Am I on the way to Bournemouth? How many stops?" He said three.

I said to the man in the carriage with me, "It has to be settled before I leave the train; you are going to hell." That man wished he had never met me. The train stopped, and I had to get out. I said, "What are you going to do?"

He answered, "I will make Him my own."

We are of the incorruptible Word of God that lives and abides forever (1 Pet. 1:23), which made the world and brought into existence things that were not there (Acts 17:24). There was nothing made except what He made, and so I realize I am made twice. I was made first by the creation of God. The next time I was born again in a moment of time, eternally begotten. If you believe in your heart, you can begin to speak, and whatever you say will come to pass if you believe in your heart. Ask God to give you the grace to use the faith you have.

3

Faith Based upon Knowledge

Then they said to Him, "What shall we do, that we may work the works of God?" Jesus answered and said to them, "This is the work of God, that you believe in Him whom He sent."
—John 6:28–29

othing in the world glorifies God as much as simple rest of faith in what God's Word says. *"This is the work of God, that you believe."* Jesus said, *"My Father has been working until now, and I have been working"* (John 5:17). He saw the way the Father did the works; it was on the groundwork of knowledge, faith based upon knowledge. When I know Him, there are so many promises I can lay hold of, and then there is no struggle, *"for [he] who asks receives, and he who seeks finds, and to him who knocks it will be opened"* (Matt. 7:8).

Jesus lived to manifest God's glory in the earth, to show forth what God was like, so that many sons might be brought to glory (Heb. 2:10). John the Baptist came as a forerunner, testifying beforehand to the coming revelation of the Son. The Son came, and in the power of the Holy Spirit revealed faith. The living God has chosen us in the midst of His people. The power is not of us, but of God. Yes, beloved, it is the power of Another within us.

Jesus, the Son of God

In the measure we are clothed and covered and hidden in Him, His inner working is manifested. Jesus said, *"My Father has been working until now, and I have been working"* (John 5:17). Oh, the joy of knowing Him! We know if we look back on how God has taken us on. We love to shout "Hallelujah," pressed out beyond measure by the Spirit as He brings us face to face with reality, while He is dwelling in us and manifesting the works. I must know the sovereignty of His grace and the manifestation of His power. Where am I? I am in Him; He is in God. The Holy Spirit, the great Revealer of the Son, is in us for revelation to manifest the Christ of God. Therefore, let it be known to you that *"the Father who dwells in* [Christ] *does the works"* (John 14:10). *"The law of the Spirit of life in Christ Jesus has made* [us] *free from the law of sin and death"* (Rom. 8:2).

All Unbelief Is Dethroned

The Spirit working in righteousness has brought us to the place where Christ is made our Head; *"this was the Lord's doing, and it is marvelous in our eyes"* (Matt. 21:42). It is a glorious fact that we are in God's presence, possessed by Him. We are not our own; we are clothed with Another. And what for? For the deliverance of the people.

Faith Based upon Knowledge

Many can testify to the day and hour when they were delivered from sickness by a supernatural power. Some would have passed away with influenza if God had not intervened, but God stepped in with a new revelation, showing us we are born from above, born by a new power, God dwelling in us and superseding the old. *"If you ask anything in My name, I will do it"* (John 14:14). If you dare to believe, *"ask, and you will receive, that your joy may be full"* (John 16:24). *"What shall we do, that we may work the works of God?...This is the work of God, that you believe in Him whom He sent."* God is more eager to answer than we are to ask. I am speaking of faith based upon knowledge.

Testimonies to This Faith

I was healed of appendicitis, because of faith based upon the knowledge of the experience of faith. When I have ministered to others, God has met and answered according to His will. The knowledge that God will not fail us if we will only believe is in our trust and our knowledge of the power of God. The centurion had this faith when he said to Jesus, *"Speak a word, and my servant will be healed"* (Matt. 8:8). Jesus answered him, *"'Go your way; and as you have believed, so let it be done for you.' And his servant was healed that same hour"* (v. 13).

In one place where I was staying, a young man came in telling us his sweetheart was dying; there was no hope. I said, "Only believe." And this was faith based upon knowledge. I knew that what God had done for me He could do for her. We went to the house. Her sufferings were terrible to witness. I said,

"In the name of Jesus, come out of her." She cried, "Mother, Mother, I am well." Then I said that the only way to make us believe it was for her to get up and dress. Presently she came down dressed. The doctor came in and examined her carefully. He said, "This is of God; this is the finger of God." It was faith based upon knowledge.

If I were to receive a check for a thousand pounds and knew only imperfectly the character of the man who sent it, I would be careful of him. I would be careful not to rely on the money until the check was honored. Jesus, on the other hand, did great works because of His knowledge of His Father. Faith begets knowledge, fellowship, and communion. If you see imperfect faith, full of doubt, a wavering condition, it always comes because of imperfect knowledge.

> *Jesus...said, "Father...I know that You always hear Me, but because of the people who are standing by I said this, that they may believe that You sent Me."...He cried with a loud voice, "Lazarus, come forth!"* (John 11:41–43)

> *Now God worked unusual miracles by the hands of Paul, so that even handkerchiefs or aprons were brought from his body to the sick, and the diseases left them and the evil spirits went out of them.* (Acts 19:11–12)

> *For our citizenship is in heaven, from which we also eagerly wait for the Savior, the Lord Jesus Christ, who will transform our lowly body that it may be conformed to His glorious*

*body, according to the working by which He is
able even to subdue all things to Himself.*
(Phil. 3:20–21)

How God has cared for me and blessed me these
twelve years, giving me such a sense of His presence!
How bountiful God is when we depend upon Him!
He gives us enough to spare for others. Lately God
has enabled me to gain victory along new lines, an
indwelling—Holy Spirit attitude in a new way. As we
meet Him, the glory falls immediately. The Holy
Spirit has the latest news from the Godhead and has
designed for us the right place at the right time.
Events happen in a remarkable way. You drop in
where the need is.

I have come across several mental cases lately.
How difficult they are naturally, but how easy for
God to deal with. One lady came saying, "Just over
the way there is a young man terribly afflicted, with
no rest day or night." I went with a very imperfect
knowledge as to what I had to do, but in the weak
places God helps our infirmities. I rebuked the demon in the name of Jesus, and then I said, "I'll come
again tomorrow." The next day when I went, he was
quite well and with his father in the field.

Here is another case. Fifty miles away there was
a fine young man, twenty-five years of age. He had
lost his reason, could have no communication with
his mother, and was always wandering up and down.
I knew God was waiting to bless. I cast out the demon
power and heard long after that he had become quite
well. Thus the blessed Holy Spirit takes us on from
one place to another. So many things happen; I live in
heaven on earth. Just the other day, at Coventry, God

relieved the people. Thus He takes us on and on and on. Do not wait for inspiration if you are in need; the Holy Spirit is here, and you can have perfect deliverance.

I was taken to three persons, one in care of an attendant. As I entered the room, there was a terrible din and quarreling. It was such a noise it seemed as if all the powers of hell were stirred. I had to wait for God's time. The Holy Spirit rose in me at the right time, and the three were delivered and at night were singing praises to God. There had to be activity and testimony. Let it be known to you that this Man Christ is the same today. Which man? God's Man who has to have the glory, power, and dominion. *"For He must reign till He has put all enemies under His feet"* (1 Cor. 15:25). When He reigns in you, you know how to obey and how to work in conjunction with His will, His power, His light, and His life. When we have faith based upon knowledge, we know He has come. *"You shall receive power when the Holy Spirit has come upon you"* (Acts 1:8). We are in the experience of it.

Sometimes a live word comes to me. In the presence of a need, a revelation of the Spirit comes to my mind, "You will be loosed." Loosed now? It looks like presumption, but God is with the man who dares to stand upon His Word. I remember, for instance, a person who had not been able to smell anything for four years. I said, "You will smell now if you believe." This stirred another who had not smelled for twenty years. I said, "You will smell tonight." She went about smelling everything and was quite excited. The next day she gave her testimony.

Another came and asked, "Is it possible for God to heal my ears?" The eardrums had been removed. I said, "Only believe." She went down into the audience in great distress; others were healed, but she could not hear. The next night she came again. She said, "I am going to believe tonight." The glory fell. The first time she came feeling; the second time she came believing.

At one place there was a man anointed for a rupture. He came the next night and rose in the meeting saying, "This man is an impostor. He is deceiving the people. He told me last night I was healed; I am worse than ever today." I spoke to the evil power that held the man and rebuked it, telling the man he was indeed healed. He was a mason. Next day he testified to lifting heavy weights and that God had met him. *"By His stripes we are healed....And the LORD has laid on Him the iniquity of us all"* (Isa. 53:5–6). He was against the Word of God, not me.

"'What shall we do, that we may work the works of God?' Jesus answered and said to them, 'This is the work of God, that you believe in Him whom He sent.'" Anything else? Yes. He took our infirmities and healed all our diseases. I myself am a marvel of healing. If I fail to glorify God, the stones would cry out.

> Salvation is for all,
> Healing is for all.
> The baptism of the Holy Spirit
> Is for all.

Consider *"yourselves to be dead indeed unto sin, but alive unto God"* (Rom. 6:11). By His grace get the victory every time. It is possible to live a holy life.

Smith Wigglesworth on Faith

He breaks the power of canceled sin,
He sets the prisoner free;
His blood can make the foulest clean,
His blood avails for me.

*"What shall we do, that we may work the works
of God?" Jesus answered and said to them,
"This is the work of God, that you believe
in Him whom He sent."*

4

Faith Is the Victory

e may be in a very low ebb of the tide, but it is good to be in a place where the tide can rise. I pray that the Holy Spirit will so have His right-of-way that there will not be one person here who will not be moved upon by the Spirit of God. Everything depends upon our being filled with the Holy Spirit. And there is nothing you can come short of if the Holy Spirit is the prime mover in your thoughts and life, for He has a plan greater than ours. If He can only get us in readiness for His plan to be worked out, it will be wonderful.

Faith to Believe God

Hebrews 11:1–10 is a very remarkable passage of Scripture for us when we are talking about faith. Everything depends upon our believing God. If we are saved, it is only because God's Word says so. We cannot rest upon our feelings. We cannot do anything without a living faith. It is surely God Himself who comes to us in the person of His beloved Son and so strengthens us that we realize that our bodies are surrounded by His power and are being lifted into the almightiness of His power. All things are possible for us in God.

The purpose of God for us is that we might be on the earth for a manifestation of His glory, that every time satanic power is confronted, God might be able to say of us as He did of Job, "What do you think about him?" (See Job 1:8.) God wants us so manifested in His divine plan in the earth that Satan will have to hear God. The joy of the Lord can be so manifested in us that we will be so filled with God that we will be able to rebuke the power of the devil.

God has showed me in the night watches that everything that is not of faith is sin (Rom. 14:23). I have seen this in the Word so many times. God wants very much to bring us into harmony with His will so that we will see that if we do not come right up to the Word of God to believe it all, there is something in us that is not purely sanctified to accept the fullness of His Word. Many people are putting their human wisdom right in the place of God, and God is not able to give the best because the human is confronting God in such a way. God is not able to get the best through us until the human will is dissolved.

"Faith is the substance of things hoped for" (Heb. 11:1). I want to speak about *"substance"*; it is a remarkable word. Many people come to me and say, "I want things to be tangible. I want something to appeal to my human reasoning." My response to this is that everything that you cannot see is eternal. Everything you can see is natural and fades away. Everything you see now will fade away and will be consumed, but what you cannot see, what is more

real than you, is the substance of all things: God in the human soul, mightier than you by a million times.

Beloved, we have to go out and be faced with all evil powers. Even your own heart, if it is not entirely immersed in the Spirit, will deceive you. So I am praying that there will not be a vestige of your human nature that will not be clothed upon with the power of the Spirit. I pray that the Spirit of the living God may be so imparted to your heart that nothing will in any way be able to move you. *"Faith is the substance of things hoped for, the evidence of things not seen"* (Heb. 11:1).

Faith to Place Jesus in You

God has mightily blessed to me 1 Peter 1:23: *"Having been born again, not of corruptible seed but incorruptible, through the word of God which lives and abides forever."* We read, *"In the beginning was the Word, and the Word was with God, and the Word was God"* (John 1:1). Then we read that *"the Word became flesh and dwelt among us, and we beheld His glory, the glory as of the only begotten of the Father, full of grace and truth"* (v. 14). And He is manifested in the midst of us. His disciples went out and manifested that they had seen and touched Him, the Word of Life.

If you turn to 2 Peter 1:4, you will find that we have received His divine nature, which is infinite power, infinite knowledge, infinite pleasure, and infinite revelation. People are missing it because we have failed to apply it. However, God is making up a people who will have to be firstfruits. By simple faith, you entered in and claimed your rights and became Christians, being born again because you believed. But there is something different in knowing God, in having fellowship with Him; there are heights and depths in this wonderful blessing in the knowledge of Him. Everybody can see Jacob, but do not forget, beloved, that God changed Jacob into Israel. The Holy Spirit wants everybody to see the unveiling of Jesus. The unveiling of Jesus is to take away yourself and to place Him in you, to take away all your human weakness and put within you that wonderful Word of eternal power and of eternal life that makes you believe that all things are possible.

Examples of Faith

A man traveled with me from Montreal to Vancouver and then on ship to New Zealand. He was a dealer of race horses. It seemed he could not leave me. He was frivolous and talked about races, but he could not keep his end of the conversation up. I did not struggle to keep my end up because mine is a living power. No person who has Jesus as the inward power of his body needs to be trembling when Satan comes around. All he has to do is to stand still and see the salvation of the Lord.

This man entered into a good deal of frivolity and talk of this world. Coming upon a certain island of the Fiji group, we all went out, and God gave me wonderful liberty in preaching. The man came back afterwards; he did not go to his racing and card-playing chums. He came stealing back to the ship, and with tears in his eyes, he said, "I am dying. I have been bitten by a snake." His skin had turned to a dark green, and his leg was swollen. "Can you help me?" he asked. If we only knew the power of God!

If we are in a place of substance, of reality, of ideal purpose, it is not human; we are dealing with almightiness. I have a present God, I have a living faith, and the living faith is the Word. The Word is life, and the Word is equipment, and the Lord is *"the same yesterday, today, and forever"* (Heb. 13:8). Placing my hand upon the serpent bite, I said, "In the name of Jesus, come out!" He looked at me, and the tears came. The swelling went down before his eyes, and he was perfect in a moment.

Yes, *"faith is the substance of things hoped for, the evidence of things not seen"* (Heb. 11:1). Faith is what came into me when I believed. I was born of the incorruptible Word by the living virtue, life, and personality of God. I was instantly changed from nature to grace. I became a servant of God, and I became an enemy of unrighteousness.

The Holy Spirit wants us to clearly understand that we are a million times bigger than we know. Every Christian has no conception of what he is. My heart is so big that I want to look in your faces and tell you if you only knew what you had, your body would scarcely be able to contain you. Oh, that God would so bring us into divine attractiveness by His almightiness that all our bodies would wake up to resurrection force, to the divine, inward flow of eternal power coursing through the human frame.

Let us read in Ephesians:

> But to each one of us grace was given according to the measure of Christ's gift. Therefore He says: "When He ascended on high, He led

captivity captive, and gave gifts to men."...And He Himself gave some to be apostles, some prophets, some evangelists, and some pastors and teachers, for the equipping of the saints for the work of ministry, for the edifying of the body of Christ, till we all come to the unity of the faith and of the knowledge of the Son of God, to a perfect man, to the measure of the stature of the fullness of Christ. (Eph. 4:7–8, 11–13)

God took you into His pavilion and began to clothe you and give you the gifts of the Spirit. He did this so that in that ministry by the power of God you would bring all the church into the perfect possession of the fullness of Christ. Oh, the wonder of it! Oh, the adaptability of His equipment!

Interpretation of Tongues

God has designed it. In the pavilion of His splendor, with the majesty of His glory He comes and, touching human weakness, beautifies it in the Spirit of holiness until the effectiveness of this wonderful sonship is made manifest in us, until we all become the edification of the fullness of Christ.

I believe God wants something to be in you that could never be unless you cease to be for yourself. God wants you to be for Him, to be for everybody. But, oh, to have the touch of God! Beloved, the Holy Spirit is the Comforter. The Holy Spirit did not come to speak of Himself, but He came to unveil Him who said, *"Take My yoke upon you and learn from Me, for I am gentle and lowly in heart, and you will find rest for your souls"* (Matt. 11:29). The Holy Spirit came to thrill you with resurrection power, and He came so that you would be anointed with fresh oil that overflows in the splendor of His almightiness. Then right through you will come forth a river of divine anointing that will sustain you in the bitterest place. It will give life to the deadest formality and say to the weak, "Be strong," and to them who have no might, "The Lord of Hosts is here to comfort you." God wants us to be like the rising of the sun, filled with the rays of heaven, all the time beaming forth the gladness of the Spirit of the Almighty. Possibility is the greatest thing of your life.

I came to the tent yesterday afternoon. No one but myself could understand my feelings. Was it emotion? No, it was an inward inspiration to find hearts that God had touched and that had met me with such love that it was almost more than I could bear. I have to thank God for it and take courage that He has been with me in the past, and He will be with me in the future. I am satisfied that love is the essential. Love is of God; no, more than this, love is God. Love is the Trinity working in the human to break it up so that it may be displaced with God's fullness.

When I was ministering to the sick, a man came among the crowd. If you had seen him, your heart would have ached for him. He was shriveled and weakened; his cheek bones were sticking out, his eyes sunk, and his neck all shriveled. He was just a form of a man. His coat hung on him as you would put it on some stick. He whispered, for he could only speak with a weak voice, "Can you help me?"

I asked "What is it?" He said that he had had cancer of his stomach, and on the operation table they had taken away the cancer. But in the operation they made it so that the man could not swallow.

He said, "I have tried to take the juice of a cherry today, but it would not go down." Then he pulled out a tube about nine inches long, which had a cup at the top. He whispered, "I have a hole in my stomach. As I pour liquid in, my stomach receives that. I have been living this way for three months."

You could call it a shadow of life he was living. Could I help him? Look! This Book can help anybody. This Book is the essence of life. God moves as you believe. This Book is the Word of God. Could I help him? I said, "On the authority of this Word, this night you will have a big supper."

But he said he could not eat. "Do as I tell you," I answered.

"How can it be?"

"It is time," I said, "to go and eat a good supper." He went home and told his wife.

She could not understand it. She said, "You cannot eat. You cannot swallow."

But he whispered, "The man said I had to do it." He got hungry and hungrier and ventured, "I will try it." His wife got his supper ready. He got a mouth full, and it went down just as easy as possible. He went on eating food until he was filled up. Then he and his wife had one of the best times of their lives. The next morning he was so full of joy because he had eaten again. He looked down out of curiosity to see the hole and found that God had closed it up!

But you ask, Can He do it for me? Yes, if you believe it. Faith is the victory. Here I am, so thankful this morning. Thirty years ago this body you see was sick and helpless and dying. God, in an instant, healed me. I will be sixty-five years old in a day or two, and I am so free and healthy; oh, it is wonderful! There are people in this place who ought to be healed in a moment, people who ought to receive the Holy Spirit in a moment. The power of possibility is in the reach of every man. The Holy Spirit is full of the rising tide. Every one of us can be filled to overflowing. God is here with His divine purpose to change our weakness into mighty strength and faith. The Word of God, oh, brother, sister, have you got it? It is marrow to your bones. It is anointing. It is resurrection from every weakness, it is life from the dead.

If there is anything I want to shake you loose from, it is having a word of faith without the power of it. What are we here for? Surely we are not to hear only; we are to obey. Obedience is better than sacrifice (1 Sam. 15:22). God the Holy Spirit wants to give us such a revelation of Christ that we would go away as men who had seen the king. We would go away with our faces lit up with the brilliancy of heaven.

How many are willing to believe? The people who would like God to know they are in sincerity and they will do whatever His Spirit tells them, cry to God until you have all you want. Let God have His way. Touch God now. Faith is the victory.

5

The Faith of God

ou know, beloved, there are many wonderful treasures in the storehouse of God that we have not yet gotten to. But praise God, we have the promise in Corinthians: *"Eye has not seen, nor ear heard, nor have entered into the heart of man the things which God has prepared for those who love Him"* (1 Cor. 2:9).

Interpretation of Tongues

Fear not, neither be dismayed, for the God who has led, will descend upon you, will surely carry you where you cannot go. But to this end He has called you out to take you on, to move upon you with a divine anointing of the Spirit, so that you should not be entertained by nature, but caught up with Him to hear His words, to speak His truth, to have His mind, to know His will, to commune and be still, to see Him who is invisible, to be able to pour out to others the great stream of life, and to quicken everything wherever it moves. For the Spirit is not given by measure, but He is given to us by faith, the measureless measure, that we may know Him and the power of His resurrection in the coming day. And now is the day set for us that is the opening for the coming day.

The Foundation of Faith

I pray to God that there may be within us a deep hunger and thirst with the penetration that is centered entirely upon the axle of Him, for surely He is all and in all.

Now, you will clearly see that God wants to bring us to a foundation. If we are ever going to make any progress in the divine life, we will have to have a real foundation. And there is no foundation except the foundation of faith for us.

All our movements, and all that ever will come to us that is of any importance, will be because we have a Rock. And if you are on the Rock, no powers can move you. And today we need to have our faith firmly built upon the Rock. In any area or principle of your faith, you must have something established in you to bring it forth. And there is no establishment outside God's Word for you. Everything else is sand. Everything else will break apart.

If you build on anything else—on imaginations, sentimentality, any feelings, or any special joy—but the Word of God, it will mean nothing without the foundation, and the foundation will have to be in the Word of God.

I was once going on a tram to Blackpool. It is a fashionable resort, and many people go there because of the high tides and the wonderful sights they see as the ocean throws up its large, massive mountain of sea. When we were going on the tram, I looked over and said to a builder, "The men are building those houses upon the sands."

"Oh," he said, "you don't know. You are not a builder. Don't you know that we can pound that sand until it becomes like rock?"

I said, "Nonsense!" I saw the argument was not going to profit, so I dropped it. By and by we reached Blackpool, where the mountainous waves come over. I was looking and taking notice of so many things. I saw a row of houses that had fallen flat, and drawing the attention of this man I said, "Oh, look at those houses. See how flat they are." He forgot our previous conversation and said, "You know here we have very large tides, and these houses, being on the sands when the floods came, fell."

We must have something better than sand, and everything is sand except the Word. There isn't anything that will remain. We are told that heaven and earth will be melted with fervent heat (2 Pet. 3:10). But we are told the Word of God will be forever, and not one jot or tittle of the Word of God will fail (Matt. 5:18). And if there is anything that is satisfying me today more than another, it is, *"Your word is settled in heaven"* (Ps. 119:89). And another passage in Psalm 138 says, *"You have magnified Your word above all Your name"* (v. 2). The very establishment for me is the Word of God. It is not on any other line.

Let us come to the principle of the matter. If you turn to John's gospel, you will find a wonderful passage there. It is worth our notice and great consideration:

> *In the beginning was the Word, and the Word was with God, and the Word was God. He was*

*in the beginning with God. All things were
made through Him, and without Him nothing
was made that was made.* (John 1:1–3)

There we have the foundation of all things,
which is the Word. It is a substance; it is a power. It
is more than relationship; it is personality. It is a divine injunction to every soul that enters into this
privilege to be born of this Word. What it means to
us will be very important for us. For remember, it is
a *"substance"*; it is an *"evidence of things not seen"*
(Heb. 11:1). It brings about what you cannot see. It
brings forth what is not there, and it takes away
what is there and substitutes for it.

God took the Word and made the world of the
things that did not appear. And we live in the world
that was made by the Word of God, and it is inhabited
by millions of people. And you say it is a substance.
Jesus, the Word of God, made it with the things that
did not appear. And nothing has been made that has
not been made by the Word. And when we come to
the truth of what that Word means, we will be able
not only to build, but also to know, not only to know,
but also to have. For if there is anything helping me
today more than anything else, it is the fact that I am
living in facts; I am moving in facts; I am in the
knowledge of the principles of the Most High.

The Wisdom of Divine Revelation

God is making manifest His power. God is a reality and is proving His mightiness in the midst of
us. And as we open ourselves to divine revelation
and get rid of all things that are not of the Spirit,

then we will understand how mightily God can take us on in the Spirit, move the things that appear, and bring the things that do not appear into prominence.

Oh, the riches, the depths of the wisdom of the Most High God! Jabez knew that there were divine principles that we needed to know, and he said, *"Enlarge* [me]*"* (1 Chron. 4:10). David knew that there was a mightiness beyond and within, and he said, *"He has dealt bountifully with me"* (Ps. 13:6), knowing that all the springs that were in him and had made his face to shine had come from God. And God is an inward witness of a power, of a truth, of a revelation, of an inward presence, of a divine knowledge. He is! He is!

Then I must understand. I must clearly understand. I must have a basis of knowledge for everything that I say. We must never say what we think; we must say what we know. Any man can think. You must be beyond the thinking. You must have the knowledge. And God wants to make us so loyal to Him that He unveils Himself. He rolls the clouds away; the mists disappear at His presence. He is almighty in His movements. God has nothing small. He is all large, an immensity of wisdom, unfolding the grandeur of His design or plan for humanity so that humanity may sink into insignificance, and the mightiness of the mighty power of God may move upon us until we are the sons of God with power, in revelation and might and strength in the knowledge of God. Oh, this wonderful salvation! Now let us think about it, it is so beautiful. Seeing then that God took the Word—what was the Word? The Word was Jesus. The Word became flesh and dwelt among us. And we beheld and saw the glory of God (John 1:14).

John has a wonderful passage on this that may lead us to edification at this moment. It is very powerful in its revelation to me as often as I gaze into the perfect law of liberty.

> *That which was from the beginning, which we have heard, which we have seen with our eyes, which we have looked upon, and our hands have handled, concerning the Word of life; the life was manifested, and we have seen, and bear witness, and declare to you that eternal life which was with the Father and was manifested to us; that which we have seen and heard we declare to you, that you also may have fellowship with us; and truly our fellowship is with the Father and with His Son Jesus Christ.* (1 John 1:1–3)

Oh, beloved, He is the Word! He is the principle of God. He is the revelation sent forth from God. All fullness dwelt in Him. We have all received a grand word of His fullness, and grace for grace.

In weakness, strength, poverty, and wealth is this Word! It is a flame of fire. It may burn in your bones. It may move in every tissue of your body. It may bring out of you so forcibly the plan and purpose and life of God until you cease to be, for God has taken you.

Born Again with Power

It is a fact that we may be taken, hallelujah! into all the knowledge of the wisdom of God. Then I want to build, if I am created anew, for it is a great creation. It took nine months to bring us forth into the world after we were conceived, but it only takes one moment to beget us as sons. The first formation was a long period of nine months. The second formation is a moment, an act, a faith, for *"he who believes... has"* (John 3:36). As you receive Him, you are begotten, not made.

Oh, the fact that I am begotten again is wonderful! I am begotten of the same seed that begot Him. Remember, as He was conceived in the womb by the Holy Spirit, so we were conceived the moment we believed and became sons of God with promise.

Oh, how the whole creation groans for sonship! (See Romans 8:22.) There is a passage in Romans, and I think it would help us to read it. Some knowledge of sonship is needed; it is a beautiful word. I have so often looked at it with pleasure, for it is such a pleasure to me to read the Word of God. Oh, the hidden treasures there are! What a feast to have the Word of God! *"Man shall not live by bread alone, but by every word of God"* (Luke 4:4). How we need the Word! The Word is life.

> *Concerning His Son Jesus Christ our Lord, who was born of the seed of David according to the flesh, and declared to be the Son of God with power according to the Spirit of holiness, by the resurrection from the dead.* (Rom. 1:3–4)

Oh, what a climax of beatitudes is here! How beautiful! God, breathe upon us this holy, inward way after His passion. Hear it: *"Declared to be the Son of God with power."*

Sons must have power. We must have power with God, power with man. We must be above all the world. We must have power over Satan and power over the evils. I want you just for a moment to think with me because it will help you with this thought. You can never make evil pure. Anything that is evil never becomes pure in that sense. There is no such a thing as ever transforming impurity into purity. The carnal mind is never subject to the will of God and cannot be (Rom. 8:7). There is only one thing for it; it must be destroyed. But I want you to go with me to when God cast out what was not pure. I want you to think about Satan in the glory with all the chances, and nothing spoiled him but his pride. And pride is an awful thing—pride in the heart, thinking we are something when we are nothing, building up a human constitution out of our own.

Oh yes, it is true the devil is always trying to make you think about what you are. You never find God doing it. It is always Satan who comes around and says, "What a wonderful address you gave! How wonderful you did that, and how wonderful you prayed and sang that song." It is all of the devil. There is not an atom of God in it, not from beginning to end. And if we only knew how much better we could preach, if we only would not miss the revelation. And Paul, in order that he might never miss the revelation, said, "Therefore I have never ceased; I have kept the faith." (See 2 Timothy 4:7.)

Oh, the vision is so needed today. It is more necessary than anything that man should have the visions of God. The people have always perished when there is no vision (Prov. 29:18 KJV). God wants us to have visions and revelations and manifestations. You cannot have the Holy Spirit without having revelations. You cannot have the Holy Spirit without being turned into another nature. It was the only credential by which Joshua and Caleb could enter the land, the fact that they were of another spirit. (See Numbers 14:30.) And we must live in an anointing, in a power, in a transformation, and in a divine attainment where we cease to be, where God becomes enthroned so richly.

Interpretation of Tongues

It is He! He came forth and emptied Himself of all, but love brought to us the grace and then offered up Himself to purge us so that we might be entire and free from all things. We would then see Him who was invisible and changed by the power that is divine and be lost to everything but the immensity of the mightiness of a God-likeness, for we must be sons of God with promise in the world.

We must be—we must be! We must not say, "It is not for me." Oh, no; we must say, "It is for us."

And God cast Satan out. Oh, I do thank God for that. Yes, beloved, but God could not have cast him out if he had even been equal of power. I tell you, beloved, we can never bind the strong man until we are in the place of binding. I thank God that Satan had to come out. Yes, and how did he come out? By the Word of God's power. And, beloved, if we get to know and understand the principles of our inheritance by faith, we will find out Satan will always be cast out by the same power that cast him out in the beginning. He will be cast out to the end because Satan has not become more holy but more vile.

If you think about the last day upon earth, you will find out that the greatest war—not Armageddon, but the war beyond that—will be between the hosts of Satan and the hosts of God. And how will it take place? With swords, dynamite, or any human power? No! It will take place by the brightness of His presence, the holiness of His holiness, the purity of His purity; where darkness cannot remain, where sin cannot stand, where only holiness and purity will remain. All else will flee from the presence of God into the abyss forever.

And God has saved us with this Word of power over the powers of sin. I know there is a teaching and a need of teaching of the personality of the presence of the fidelity of the Word of God with power. And we need to eat and drink of this Word. We need to feed upon it in our hearts. We need that holy revelation that ought always to take away the mists from our eyes and reveal Him.

Always Advancing

Beloved, don't forget that every day must be a day of advancement. If you have not made any advancement since yesterday, in a measure you are a backslider. There is only one way for you between Calvary and the glory, and it is forward. It is every day forward. It is no day back. It is advancement with God. It is cooperation with Him in the Spirit.

Beloved, we must see these things, because if we live on the same plane day after day, the vision is stale; the principles lose their earnestness. But we must be like those who are catching the vision of the Master day by day. And we must make inroads into every passion that would interfere, and we must bring everything to the slaughter that is not holy.

The Faith of God

For in these days God wants us to know that He wishes to seat us on high. Don't forget it.

The principles remain with us—if we will only obey—to seat us on high. Hallelujah! And let us still go on building because we must build this morning. We must know our foundation. We must be able to take the Word of God and make it clear to people, because we will be confronted with evil powers.

An Example of God's Faith

I am continually confronted with things that God must clear away. Every day something comes before me that has to be dealt with along these lines. For instance, when I was at Cazadero seven or eight years ago, among the first people that came to me in those meetings was a man who was completely deaf. And every time we had the meeting—suppose I was rising up to say a few words—this man would take his chair from the ordinary row and place it right in front of me. And the devil used to say, "Now you are done." I said, "No, I am not done. It is finished."

The man was as deaf as possible for those three weeks. And then in the meeting, as we were singing, this man became tremendously disturbed as though he were in a storm. He looked in every direction, and he became like someone who had almost lost his mind. And then he took a leap. He started on the run and went out among the people and right up one of the hills. When he got about sixty yards away, he heard singing. And the Lord said, "Your ears are open." He came back, and we were still singing. That stopped our singing. And then he told us that when his ears were opened, he could not understand what it was. There was such a tremendous noise he could not understand it. He thought something had happened to the world, and so he ran out of the meeting. Then, when he got away, he heard singing.

Oh, the devil said for three weeks, "You cannot do it." I said, "It is done!" As though God would ever forget! As though God could ever forget! As if it were possible for God ever to ignore our prayers!

Receiving God's Glory

The most trying time is the most helpful time. Most preachers say something about Daniel and about the Hebrew children, Shadrach, Meshach, and Abednego, and especially about Moses when he was tried and in a corner. Beloved, if you read the Scriptures, you will never find anything about the easy times. All the glories came out of hard times.

And if you are to be really reconstructed, it will be in a hard time. It won't be in a singing meeting, but at a time when you think all things are dried up, when you think there is no hope for you and you have passed up everything. That is the time that God makes the man. It is when you are tried by fire that God purges you, takes the dross away, and brings forth the pure gold. Only melted gold is minted. Only soft wax receives the seal. Only broken, contrite hearts receive the mark as the Potter turns us on His wheel, shaped and burned to take and keep the heavenly mold, the stamp of God's pure gold.

We must have the stamp of our blessed Lord, who was marred more than any man. And when He touched human weakness, it was reconstructed. He spoke out of the depths of trial and mockery and became the Initiator of a world's redemption. Man never spoke as He spoke! He was full of order and made all things move until the people said, "We never saw anything like this." He is truly the Son of God with power, with blessing, with life, and with maturity, and He can take the weakest and make them into strength.

God Can Fill You Now

God is here now in power, in blessing, in might, and saying to you, my brother, and to you, my sister, "What is it? What is your request?"

Oh, He is so precious; He never fails; He is so wonderful! He always touches the needy place. He is so gentle; He never breaks the bruised reed. He is so rich in His mighty benevolence that He makes the smoking flax to flame (Isa. 42:3).

May God move us now to see that He must have a choice from us. Oh, how precious He is! There is no passage so precious to me as when He said, *"I have desired to eat this Passover with you before I suffer"* (Luke 22:15).

Oh, that lovely, benevolent, wonderful Jesus! Before the garden experience, knowing about the cross and Gethsemane, there the love of Jesus, that holy Jesus, could say, *"With fervent desire"* (v. 15). It was the joy that was set before Him (Heb. 12:2). Will it be missed? Is it possible for the joy that was set before Him—to make us fully matured saints of God, with power over the powers of the enemy, filled with the might of His Spirit—to be missed?

Surely this is our God, for there is no God who answers like this. Let me entreat you right now to pay any price. Never mind what it costs; it is worth it all to have His smile, to have His presence—truly, more than that—to have the same desire that He had to win others for Him.

When I see His great desire to win me, I say, "Lord, remold me like that. Make me have the desire of salvation for others at any cost." Thank God He went through. He did not look back. He went right on.

You never need to be afraid of joining yourself to this Nazarene, for He is always a King. When He was dying, He was a King. Yes, if ever there was any man who spoke in tongues, Jesus spoke in tongues, for there was no interpretation. And if any man ever spoke truth, He spoke the truth when He said, *"It is finished"* (John 19:30).

Thank God it is finished. And I know, because it is finished, that everything is mine. Thank God everything is mine: things in heaven, things in earth, things under the earth. He is all power over all. He is in all. He is through all. Thank God He is for all.

And I say to you, without contradiction, that Jesus has so much more for you than you have any conception of. Just like the two sons of Zebedee—did they know what they asked? Certainly they had no conception of what they asked.

> *But Jesus...said, "...Are you able to drink the cup that I am about to drink, and be baptized with the baptism that I am baptized with?" They said to Him, "We are able."* (Matt. 20:22)

Were they able? No, but it was their hearts. Have a big heart! Have a big yes! Have a big "I will!" Have a great desire, though you are blind to what is to follow.

And the sons of Zebedee also wondered what He had. I believe that all believers want the same. Did they drink? Yes, He said they would. Did they see His baptism? Yes, He said they would. But they had no idea what it meant, what the cup was. But the cup was drunk to the dregs. Yes, His cup was different. But because of His cup, our cup runs over (Ps. 23:5). Oh, *"surely goodness and mercy shall follow [you]"* (v. 6). Your cup runs over. There may be many cups before the cup is full. But oh, hallelujah anyway, only let it be His will and His way, not my way. Oh, for His way only, and His plan, His will only!

Let the mantle fall from Him onto you today. *"If you see me when I am taken from you, it shall be"* (2 Kings 2:10). And Elisha kept his eye on Elijah. The mantle is to fall, the mantle of power, the mantle of blessing.

And I ask you now, seeing that you have this spiritual revelation in the body, in the earthly tabernacle, what are you going to do? If the body is yielded sufficiently until it perfectly becomes the temple of the Spirit, then the fullness will flow, and the life will be yielded to you and given to you as you have need of it. May God mold us all to believe it is possible now not only for the rivers, but also the mightiness of His boundless ocean to flow through us.

You should do as you are led to do. No pressure ought to be needed for you as you see your need before God and know He is here to supply your need. Therefore, why should we have to be entreated to seek the best of all when God is waiting to give without measure to each and every one? Do as the Lord leads you, and let Him direct you in whatever way.

6

Faith's Treasures

I believe that there is only one way to all the treasures of God, and it is the way of faith. There is only one principle underlying all the attributes and all the beatitudes of the mighty ascension into the glories of Christ, and it is faith. All the promises are *"Yes"* and *"Amen"* to those who believe (2 Cor. 1:20).

Let's turn to the eleventh chapter of Hebrews:

Now faith is the substance of things hoped for, the evidence of things not seen. For by it the elders obtained a good testimony. By faith we understand that the worlds were framed by the word of God, so that the things which are seen were not made of things which are visible. By faith Abel offered to God a more excellent sacrifice than Cain, through which he obtained witness that he was righteous, God testifying of his gifts; and through it he being dead still speaks. By faith Enoch was taken away so that he did not see death, "and was not found, because God had taken him"; for before he was taken he had this testimony, that he pleased God. But without faith it is impossible to please Him, for he who comes to God must believe that He is, and that He is a rewarder of those who diligently seek Him. By faith Noah, being divinely warned of things not yet seen, moved with godly fear, prepared an ark for the saving of his household, by which he condemned the world and became heir of the righteousness which is according to faith. By faith Abraham obeyed when he was called to go out to the place which he would receive as an inheritance. And he went out, not knowing where he was going. By faith he dwelt in the land of promise as in a foreign country, dwelling in tents with Isaac and Jacob, the heirs with him of the same promise; for he waited for the city which has foundations, whose builder and maker is God. (Heb. 11:1–10)

God has a way to bring us to faith, and it never comes by any human means. It always comes by divine principles. You cannot know God by nature; you get to know God by an open door of grace. He has made a way. It is a beautiful way so that all His saints can enter in by that way and find rest. The way is the way of faith; there isn't any other way. If you climb up any other way, you cannot work it out.

Say "Amen" to Jesus

There are several things that are coming before me from time to time, and I find that anything is a failure if it does not have its base right on the Rock, Christ Jesus. He is the only way, the truth, and the life (John 14:6). But praise God, He is the truth; He is the life; and His Word is Spirit and life-giving. And when we understand it in its true order to us, we find that it is not only the Word of life, but it quickens, opens, fills, moves, changes, and brings us into a place where we dare to say, "Amen!" There is a lot in an amen. I find you can have zeal without faith. And I find you can have any amount of things without faith. The following examples show the difference between the amen of faith and having zeal or other emotions without faith.

As I looked into the twelfth chapter of the Acts of the Apostles, I found that the people who were waiting all night praying for Peter to come out of prison had zeal, but they did not have faith. (See Acts 12:3–17.) They were so zealous that they even allowed themselves to eat only unleavened bread, and they prayed. It seems as if there is much that could be commended to us from this passage, but there is one thing missing. It is faith. You will find that Rhoda had more faith than all the rest of them. When the knock came at the door, she ran to it, and the moment she heard Peter's voice she ran back again with joy, saying that Peter stood before the gate.

And all the people said, "You are mad. It isn't so." And she made mention of what she saw. The people had no faith at all. But they said, "Well, God has perhaps sent an angel."

But Rhoda said, "It is Peter." And Peter continued knocking. They went and found it was so. They had zeal but no faith. And I believe there is quite a difference.

God wants to bring us into an activity where we will take hold of God in a living way. We need to rest and always see the plan of God.

There was such a difference between Zacharias and Mary. Zacharias and Elizabeth definitely wanted a son, but even when the angel came and told Zacharias that he would be the father of a son, he was full of unbelief. And the angel said, *"You will be mute and not able to speak...because you did not believe"* (Luke 1:20). But look at Mary. When the angel came to Mary, she said, *"Let it be to me according to your word"* (Luke 1:38). This was the beginning of the amen, and the presentation of the amen was when she nursed Jesus.

Believe that there can be a real amen in your life that can come to pass. And God wants us to have the amen that never knows anything else other than amen: an inward amen, a mighty moving amen, a God-likeness amen. This amen is what says, "It is," because God has spoken. It cannot be otherwise. It is impossible to be otherwise.

Changed by God

Beloved, I see all the plan of life where God comes in and vindicates His power and makes His presence felt. It is not by crying or groaning. It is because we believe. And yet, I have nothing to say about it except that sometimes it takes God a long time to bring us through the groaning and crying before we can believe.

I know this as clearly as I know anything, that no man in this place can change God. You cannot change Him. There is a very good passage in Charles Finney's lectures, and it says, "Can a man who is full of sin and all kinds of ruin in his life change God when he comes out to pray?" No, it is impossible.

But as this man labors in prayer and groans and travails, because his tremendous sin is weighing him down, he becomes broken in the presence of God. When he is properly melted in perfect harmony with the divine plan of God, then God can work in that clay. God could not do so before.

Prayer changes hearts, but it never changes God. God is the same today and forever; He is always full of love, full of entreaty, and full of helpfulness. If you always come into the presence of God, you can have what you come for. You can take it away and use it at your disposal. And there is nothing you can find in the Scriptures where God ever charges you for what you have done with what He has given you. God scolds no man, but you can come and come again, and God is willing to give if you believe.

Interpretation of Tongues

It is the living God. It is the God of power who changes things, changes us. It is He who has formed us, not we ourselves, and transformed us because it is He who comes in and makes the vessel ready for the immensity of its power working through us, transforming us into His will, His plan, for He delights in us.

God delights in us. When a man's ways please the Lord, then He makes all things to move accordingly (Prov. 16:7).

Taken Away by God

Now we come to the Word, this blessed Word, this holy Word. I want to go to a particular verse in the eleventh chapter of Hebrews:

By faith Enoch was taken away so that he did not see death, "and was not found, because God had taken him"; for before he was taken he had this testimony, that he pleased God. (Heb. 11:5)

When I was in Sweden, the Lord worked mightily there in a very blessed way. After one or two addresses, the leaders called me and said, "We have heard very strange things about you, and we would like to know whether they are true because we can see the doors are opening to you. We can see that God is with you, and God is moving, and we know that your work will be a great blessing to Sweden."

"Well," I said, "what is it?"

"Well," they said, "we have heard from good authority that you preach that you have the resurrection body." When I was in France, I had an interpreter that believed this thing, and I found out after I had preached once or twice through the interpreter that she gave her own expressions. And, of course, I did not know that she was doing this. Then I said, "Nevertheless, I will tell you what I really believe. If I had the testimony of Enoch, I would be off. I would like it, and I would like to go. Evidently no one in Sweden has the testimony of Enoch, or they would be off, because the moment Enoch had the testimony that was pleasing to God, off he went."

I pray that God will so quicken our faith, for we have a long way to go maybe before we are ready. Being taken away was in the mind of God. But remember, being taken away by God comes along the lines of holy obedience and walking with pleasure with a perfectness of God and walking together with God in the Spirit. Some others have had touches of it. It is lovely; it is delightful to think about those moments when we have walked with God and had communion with Him; when our words were lifted, and we were not made to make them, but God made them.

Oh, how wonderful is that smile of divine communication that is truly of God, where we speak to Him in the Spirit and where the Spirit lifts and lifts and lifts and takes us in! Oh, there is a place of God where God can bring us in, and I pray that God by His Spirit may move us so we will strive to be where Enoch was as he walked with God.

As Paul divinely put it by the Spirit, I don't believe that any person does not have an open door into everything that is in the Scriptures. I believe the Scriptures are for us. In order that we may apply our hearts to understand the truth, I say, "Oh, for an inroad of the mighty revolution of the human heart to break it so that God can plan afresh and make all within us say, 'Amen!'" What a blessed experience it truly is.

Supernatural Faith from God

There are two kinds of faith that God wants to let us see. I am not speaking about natural things but divine ones. There is a natural faith, and there is a saving faith. The saving faith is the gift of God. All people are born with the natural kind of faith, but this supernatural faith is the gift of God. Natural faith has its limitations. Faith that has no limitation in God can be seen in the twenty-sixth chapter of Acts. This is a very wonderful chapter. I want to define and emphasize for you the difference between the

65

natural faith and this faith that I am going to read about, beginning at the sixteenth verse:

> *But rise and stand on your feet; for I have appeared to you for this purpose, to make you a minister and a witness both of the things which you have seen and of the things which I will yet reveal to you. I will deliver you from the Jewish people, as well as from the Gentiles, to whom I now send you, to open their eyes, in order to turn them from darkness to light, and from the power of Satan to God, that they may receive forgiveness of sins and an inheritance among those who are sanctified by faith in Me.*
>
> (Acts 26:16–18)

Is that the faith of Paul? No, it is the faith that the Holy Spirit is giving. We may have much revelation of a divine plan of God through the gifts in the Lord's order, and when He speaks to me, I will begin operating in the gifts.

I see here just a touch of the gifts, where Paul, through the revelation and the open door that was given to him on the way to Damascus, saw he had the faith of salvation. I notice that as Ananias laid his hands upon him, there came a power, the promise of the Holy Spirit, that filled his body. And then I notice in that order of the Spirit, he walked in the comfort of the Holy Spirit, which is a wonderful comfort. Oh, tell me if you can, is there anything to compare to what Jesus said: "When the Holy Spirit comes, *'He will teach you all things, and bring to your remembrance all things'*" (John 14:26)? Surely this is a Comforter. Surely He is the Comforter who can bring to our memories and minds all the things that Jesus said.

And all the ways He worked is the divine plan of the Spirit to reveal to us until every one of us, without exception, tastes of this angelic, mighty touch of the heavenly as He moves upon us. The baptism of the Holy Spirit is the essential, mighty touch of revelation of the wonders, for God the Holy Spirit has no limitations along these lines. But when the soul is ready to enter into His life, there is a breaking up of fallow ground and a moving of the mists away, bringing us into the perfect day of the light of God.

And I say that Paul was moved upon by this power, and yet Jesus said to him, "As you go, you will be changed, and in the changing I will take you from revelation to revelation, open door to open door, and the accomplishment will be as My faith is committed to you."

Oh, hallelujah, there is saving faith. There is the gift of faith. It is the faith of Jesus that comes to us as we press in and on with God, a place where we can always know it is God.

An Example of Faith

I want just to put before you this difference between our faith and the faith of Jesus. Our faith comes to an end. Most people have come to a place where they have said, "Lord, I can go no further. I have gone so far; now I can go no further. I have used all the faith I have, and I just have to stop now and wait."

Well, brother, thank God that we have this faith. But there is another faith. I remember one day being in northern England and going around to see some sick people. I was taken into a house where there was a young woman lying on her bed, a very helpless case. It was a case where her reason had gone, and many things were manifested there that were satanic, and I knew it.

She was only a young woman, a beautiful child. Then the husband, who was quite a young man, came in with a baby, and he leaned over to kiss the wife. The moment he did, she threw herself over on the other side of the bed, just as a lunatic would do, with no consciousness of the presence of the husband. That was very heartbreaking. And then he took the baby and pressed the baby's lips to the mother. Again, another wild kind of thing happened. So he said to a sister who was attending her, "Have you anybody to help?"

"Oh," she said, "we have had everything."

But I said, "Have you no spiritual help?"

And her husband stormed out and said, "Help? You think that we believe in God after we have had seven weeks of no sleep and of maniac conditions? You think that we believe God? You are mistaken. You have come to the wrong house."

And then a young woman about eighteen or so just grinned at me and walked out of the door, and that finished the whole business. That brought me to a place of compassion that something had to be done for this woman; it did not matter what it was.

And then with my faith—thank God for the faith—I began to penetrate the heavens, and I was soon out of that house, I will tell you, for I never saw a man get anything from God who prayed on the earth. If you get anything from God, you will have to pray into heaven, for it is all there. If you are living on the earth and expect things from heaven, they will never come. If you want to touch the ideal, you must live in ideal principles.

And as I saw in the presence of God the limitations of my faith, there came another faith, a faith that could not be denied, a faith that took the promise, a faith that believed God's Word. And I came from that presence back again to earth, but I was not the same man under the same condition that confronted me. But in the name of Jesus, I was a man with a faith that could shake hell and move anything else.

I said, "Come out of her in the name of Jesus!" And she rolled over and fell asleep and wakened in fourteen hours, perfectly sane and perfectly whole. Oh, there is faith, the faith that is in me. And Jesus wants to bring us all into a place in line with God where we cease to be, for God must have the right of way, of thought, and of purpose. God must have the way.

Walk with God

There is a process along these lines. Enoch walked with God. That must have been all these hundreds of years as he was penetrating, and going through, and laying hold, and believing, and seeing that he had gotten to such cooperation and touch with God that things moved on earth and were moving toward heaven. And surely God came for the last time.

It was not possible for him to stop any longer. Oh, hallelujah! And I believe that God so wants to bring all of us into line with His will so that we may see signs, wonders, and various miracles and gifts of the Holy Spirit. For this is a wonderful day, the day of the Holy Spirit. It is a blessed day. If you would ask me any time, "When would you have liked to come to earth?" I would tell you, "Just now!" Oh, yes, it suits me beautifully to know that the Holy Spirit can fill the body. It is wonderful just to be a temple of the Spirit, just to manifest the glory of God! It is truly an ideal summit, and everyone can reach out his hand and have God take it and lift him up.

For the heart that is longing, God makes the longing cry. Sometimes we have an idea that there is some special thing in us that does it. No, beloved. If you have anything at all worth having, it is because God has love to give you.

I truly say that there is a plan of God for the purpose of this life. Enoch walked with God. God wants to raise the conditions of saints to walk with Him and talk with Him. I don't want to raise myself up, but it is true that if you find me not in conversation with man, I am in conversation with God.

One thing God has given to me from my youth up—and I am so thankful—is no taste or relish for any book but the Bible. And I can say before God that I have never read a book but the Bible, so I know nothing about books. As I have glanced into books, I have seen in them a little of what good people call a good book. Oh, but how much better it is to get the Book of books that contains nothing but God. If a book is commended because it has something about God in it, how much more will the Word of God be the food of the soul, the strengthening of the believer, and the building up of the human order of character with God, so that all the time the reader is being changed by the Spirit of the Lord from one state of glory into another.

This is the ideal principle of God. I have something to say about those who have gone, because Paul said, "It is better to go than to stop." But oh, I am looking forward to and believing the fact that He is coming again. And this hope in me brings me to the same place as the man of faith who looked for a city that human hands have not made. There is a city that human hands have not made, and by faith we have a right to claim our position right along as we go.

The Ideal Plan of Faith

I will turn now to Hebrews 11:6: *"But without faith it is impossible to please Him, for he who comes to God must believe that He is, and that He is a rewarder of those who diligently seek Him."*

I often think that we make great failures along these lines because of an imperfect understanding of His Word. I can see it is impossible to please God along any lines but faith, for everything that is not of faith is sin (Rom. 14:23).

God wants us all to see that the plan of faith is the ideal and principle of God. And when I remember and keep in my thoughts these beautiful words in the twelfth chapter of Hebrews, it is wonderful as I read this second verse: *"Looking unto Jesus, the author and finisher of our faith."* He is the Author of faith. Jesus became the Author of faith. God worked the plan through Him by forming the worlds and making everything that there was by the Word of

His power. Jesus Christ was the Word. God so manifested this power in the world, forming the worlds by the word of Jesus.

I see that on this divine line of principle of God, God has chosen Him, ordained Him, clothed Him, and made Him greater than all because of one principle, and on this principle only. And this principle is the love of God that gave the joy. It was the joy of the Lord to save. Because of this exceeding, abundant joy of saving the whole world, He became the Author of a living faith. And everyone is changed by this faith from grace to grace. We become divine inheritors of the promises, and we become the substance.

There is one ideal only, and that is that God is working in this holy principle of faith. It is divine.

Interpretation of Tongues

It is God installated through the flesh, quickened by His Spirit, molded by His will, until it is so in order, until God's Son could not come unless we went, for His life is in us.

Thank God for that interpretation. God's Son, this life, this faith, could not move from glory unless I move from the earth. And we should meet right in heaven. Thank God for this faith, this principle, this life, this inheritance, this truth, this eternal power working in us mightily by His Spirit!

Faith through the Word

Oh, thank God for His Word! Live it. Be moved by His Word. We will become flat and anemic and helpless without this Word. You are not any good for anything apart from the Word. The Word is everything; the Word has to become everything. When the heavens and the earth are melted away, then we will be as bright as, and brighter than, the day because of the Word of God.

We know it is quick and powerful and sharper than any two-edged sword, dividing soul and spirit, joints and marrow, and thoughts of the heart (Heb. 4:12)! God's Word is like a sword piercing through. Who could have a stiff knee if he believed in that Word?

The Word is so divinely appointed for us. Think about it. How it severs the soul and the spirit! Take it in; think it out; work it out. It is divine. See it; it is the truth.

The soul that has all the animal, all the carnal, all the selfishness, all the evil things—thank God for the truth of the Word that the soul will never inherit that place. The soul must go from where it came. It is earthly and sensual. But the two-edged sword divides it so it will have no power. And the Spirit of the life of Jesus is over it, ruling it, controlling it, and bringing it always to death.

Jesus poured out His soul unto death. Flesh and blood will not inherit the kingdom of heaven (1 Cor. 15:50). So I see it is necessary for us to have the Word of God piercing even to the dividing of soul and spirit. Then I notice the joints and marrow must have the Word of God to quicken the very marrow.

Many people in Australia came to me with double curvature of the spine, and instantly they were healed and made straight as I put hands upon them. But no man is able except the divine Son of God, and

His power moved upon these curvatures of the spine and straightened them. Oh, the mighty power of the Word of God! God must have us in these days so separated on every line as we proceed along the lines of God and see what the Word of God must bring forth. As it destroys, it brings forth. You can never live if you have never been dead. You must die if you want to live. It was the very death of Jesus that raised Him to the highest height of glory.

Every death-likeness is a likeness to the Son of God. And all the time the Word of God must quicken, flow through, and move upon us until these ideals are in us, until we move in them and live in them.

Interpretation of Tongues

The living God is lifting you out of yourself into Himself.

Come to God in Glory

We must be taken out of the ordinary and be brought into the extraordinary. We must live in a glorious position over the flesh and the devil and everything of the world. God has ordained us, clothed us within, and manifested His glory upon us so that we may be the sons with promise, of Son-likeness to Him. What an ideal! What a Savior! What an ideal Savior! And to be like Him! Oh, yes, we can be like Him. The ideal principle is for God to make us like Him.

Then I see another truth. How do you come to God? Where is God? Is He in the ceiling, in the elements, in the air, in the wind? Where is God? He who comes to God—where is He? God is in you. Oh, hallelujah! And you will find the Spirit of the living God in you, which is the prayer circle, which is the lifting power, which is the revelation element, which is the divine power that lifts you.

He who comes to God is already in the place where the Holy Spirit takes the prayers and swings them out according to the mind of the Spirit. For who has known the mind of Christ, or who is able to make intercession, except the mind of the Spirit of the living God? He makes intercession. Where is He? He is in us. Oh, this baptism of the Holy Spirit is an inward presence of the personality of God that lifts, prays, takes hold, and lives in us with a tranquillity of peace and power that rests and says, "It is all right."

God answers prayer because the Holy Spirit prays, your advocate is Jesus, and the Father is the Judge of all. There He is. Is it possible for any prayer to be missed on those lines? Let us be sure that we are in this place now.

"He who comes to God must believe that He is, and that He is a rewarder of those who diligently seek Him" (Heb. 11:6). He who comes to God must believe that God is. You cannot help it. You must believe He is already in the temple.

But some people have not yet entered into the experience because they have never come out. But God said to Abraham, "Come out, come out." (See Genesis 12:1.) And if you have never heard the voice of God telling you to come out, you may be in the wilderness a long time before you enter in. Now look at the ridiculousness of Abraham, that is, from the human viewpoint. Look at it in Hebrews 11:8: *"By faith Abraham obeyed when he was called to go out to the place which he would receive as an inheritance."* What a silly man he was! *"Not knowing where he was going"* (v. 8). Why, that was the very secret of power. Everything was there. If there is anything that I know that is worth knowing, it is what God is always teaching me about Himself.

There is something about wanting to follow God's mind until we will be what He wants us to be all the time. God has ordered it so. God has planned it so. God wills it. God has no other method or plan of saving ruined man except by man. And when man remains in the place where God has called him, so that he can be a perfect man following God's plan for him, then he will surely have reached the attitude where God has said, "Come out, for I have a place for you, and you can never reach the place without Me. But I am willing that you should be for Me so that I may be for you."

Oh, this God of grace! Oh, this willingness for God to let us see His face! Oh, this longing of my soul that cannot be satisfied without more of God! Oh, it is this, more of God, that I want! I feel that I am the youngest man in the world.

Unless God does something, I would be an awful failure. But surely He will do it. He has brought us in so that He might take us out. And God will never leave us in an unfinished plane.

It is all divine order. There is nothing wrong in the plan of God. It is all in perfect order. To think that God can make a mistake is the biggest blunder that a man makes in his life. God makes no mistakes. But when we are in the will of God, the plan works out admirably because it is divine and thought out by the almightiness of God.

Oh, beloved, have you come out yet? You say, "Out of what?" Out of what you know you didn't want to be in. Why should I answer your questions when you can answer them yourselves? It would be a waste of time. No need of going on that line. But God knows where you are and where you ought to be. Many of you heard the voice of God long ago, but still you have not obeyed. Will you come out? God says, "Come out!" But you say, "Where will I go? Where will I come out?" Come out into God, unto God, oh, hallelujah!

I think it is just about time to come out. It is such a mistake to hold on and not obey Him when you hear His voice. But when we obey, it is so sweet! So I will stop at this time because God probably has something better to teach you in the Spirit as you obey His call and obey His "Come out." God has something better for you than I can tell you. Oh, I say to you, "Come out," and I will leave you either to sit still or come out. Amen!

7

The Inheritance of Faith

here are things in this chapter that will bring a revelation of what God intends for the man who believes. The great plan of God's salvation is redemption in its fullness. I know that prayer is wonderful, and not only changes things but changes you. I know that the man of prayer can go right in and take the blessing from God; yet I tell you that if we grasp this truth that we have before us, we will find that faith is the greatest inheritance of all.

May God give us faith that will bring this glorious inheritance into our hearts, for it is true that the just will live by faith (Rom. 1:17), and do not forget that it takes a just man to live by faith. May the Lord reveal to us the fullness of this truth that God gave to Abraham.

Looking to God's Promise

For twenty-five years Abraham had the promise that God would give him a son. For twenty-five years he stood face-to-face with God on the promise, every year expecting to have a son. There was Sarah becoming weaker, and Abraham's own stamina and body were becoming frailer. Natural conditions were so changing both Sarah and him that, as far as they could see, there was no such thing as seeing their bodies bring forth fruit. And, if they had looked at their bodies as some people do theirs, they would probably have remained as they were forever. But Abraham dared not look either at Sarah or himself in that respect. He had to look at God. You cannot find anywhere that God ever failed. And He wants to bring us into that blessed place of faith, changing us into a real substance of faith, until we are so like-minded that whatever we ask, we believe we receive, and our joy becomes full because we believe. I want you to see how God covered Abraham because he believed.

Hear what God said to Abraham, and then see how Abraham acted. He was among his own people and his own kindred, and God said to him, "Come out, Abraham, come out!" And Abraham obeyed and came out, not knowing where he was going. You will never go through with God in any area except by believing Him. It is "Thus says the Lord" every time, and you will see the plan of God come right through when you dare to believe. He came right out of his own country, and God was with him. Because he believed God, God overshadowed him.

I am as confident as possible that if we could get to the place of believing God, we would not need to rely on a dog in the yard or a lock on the door. All this is unbelief. God is able to manage the whole business. It doesn't matter how many thieves are about; they cannot break through or steal where God is.

The Inheritance of Faith

I want, by the help of God, to lead you into the truth, for nothing but the truth can set you free (John 8:32). Truth can always do it. It is impossible, if God covers you with His righteousness, for anything to happen to you that is contrary to the mind of God.

When God sets His seal upon you, the devil will not dare to break it. He will not dare to break in where you are. You know what a seal is, don't you? Now, then, when God puts His seal upon you, the devil has no power there. He will not dare to break that seal and go through, and God puts His seal upon the man who believes Him.

There are two kinds of righteousness. There is a righteousness that is according to the law, the keeping of the law, but there is a better righteousness than that. You ask, "What could be better than keeping the law?" The righteousness that sees God and obeys Him in everything is better. The righteousness that believes that every prayer uttered is going to bring the answer from God is better. There is a righteousness that is made known only to the heart that knows God. There is a side to the inner man that God can reveal only to the man who believes Him.

We have many scriptural illustrations to show us how God worked with those people who believed Him. I have many definite instances in my life where God came, where God was, where God worked, and where God planned. And here is one of the greatest plans of all, where God works in this man Abraham exactly opposite to human nature. There were many good points about Sarah, but she had not reached the place. She laughed and then denied having done so (Gen. 18:12, 15). Before that, when they had waited a time and she had seen that their bodies were growing frailer, she had said, "Now it will be just as good for you to take Hagar for a wife and bring forth a son through her." (See Genesis 16:1–2.) But that was not the seed of Abraham that God had spoken about, and that caused a great deal of trouble in the house of Abraham.

There are times when you dare not take your spouse's advice. The man who walks with God can only afford to follow God's leadings, and when He leads you, it is direct and clear. The evidence is so real that every day you know that God is with you, unfolding His plan to you. It is lovely to be in the will of God.

Interpretation of Tongues

Glory to God! He is the Lord of Hosts who comes forth into the heart of the human life of man and speaks according to His divine plan. And as you live in the Spirit, you live in the process of God's mind and act according to His divine will.

Thus, there is a higher order than the natural man, and God wants to bring us into this higher order where we will believe Him. In the first place, God promised Abraham a son. Could a child be born into the world, except on the line of the natural law? It was when all natural law was finished and when there was no substance in these two persons, Abraham and Sarah, that the law of the Spirit brought forth a son. It was the law of faith in the God who had promised.

The Inheritance of Faith

Born of God

And then we are brought to the time when our blessed Lord was conceived. I hear Mary saying to the angel, *"Lord! Let it be to me according to your word"* (Luke 1:38), so that the Man Christ Jesus was brought forth along the same lines. I see before me faces I know, and I can see that these men are born, not of blood, or by the will of the flesh, but of God (John 1:13). We have the same law in our midst now: born of God! And sometimes I see that this power within us is greater when we are weak than when we are strong, and this power was greater in Abraham as days went by than when he was strong.

Looking at him, Sarah would shake her head and say, "I never saw anybody so thin and weak and helpless in my life. No, Abraham, I have been looking at you, and you seem to be going right down." But Abraham refused to look at his own body or Sarah's; he believed that the promise would happen.

Suppose you come for healing. You know as well as possible that, according to the natural life, there is no virtue in your body to give you that health. You also know that the ailment from which you suffer has so drained your life and energy that there is no help at all in you, but God says that you will be healed if you believe. It makes no difference how your body is. It was exactly the helplessness of Sarah and Abraham that brought the glorious fact that a son was born, and I want you to see what sort of a son he was.

He was the son of Abraham. His seed is the seed of the whole believing church—innumerable as the sands upon the seashore. God wants you to know that there is no limitation with Him, and He wants to bring us to a place where there will be no limitation in us. This state would be brought about by the working of the Omnipotent in the human body, working in us continually—the One who is greater than any science or any power in the world—and bringing us into the place to comprehend God and man.

I want you to see that Romans 4:16 has a great message for us all:

> *Therefore it is of faith that it might be according to grace, so that the promise might be sure to all the seed, not only to those who are of the law, but also to those who are of the faith of Abraham, who is the father of us all.*

Think about those words, *"Therefore it is of faith that it might be according to grace."* Some of you would like a touch in your bodies; some would like a touch in your spirit; some would like to be baptized in the Holy Spirit; some want to be filled with all God's power. It is there for you: *"That the blessing of Abraham might come upon the Gentiles in Christ Jesus, that we might receive the promise of the Spirit through faith"* (Gal. 3:14).

Now come on the lines of faith again. I want you to see that you can be healed if you will hear the Word. Now, some people want healing; maybe some need salvation; maybe others want sanctification and the baptism of the Spirit. The verse from Romans says it is by faith, that it might be by grace. Grace is omnipotence; it is activity, benevolence, and mercy. It is truth, perfection, and God's inheritance in the soul that can believe. God gives us a negative side. What is it? It is by faith. Grace is God. You open the door by faith, and God comes in with all you need and want. It cannot be otherwise, for it is *"of faith that it might be according to grace."* It cannot be by grace unless you say it will be so.

This is believing, and most people want healing by feeling. It cannot be. Some even want salvation on the same lines, and they say, "Oh, if only I could feel I was saved!" It will never come that way. There are three things that work together. The first is faith. Faith can always bring the second thing—a fact— and a fact can always bring the third thing—joy. So God brings you to hear the Scriptures, which can make you wise unto salvation (2 Tim. 3:15), which can open your understanding and make you so that if you will hear the truth, you will go out with what you want. Then you have power to shut the door and power to open the door.

Dare to Believe!

Let us now look step-by-step at another verse that is mightier still, and you will find it is very wonderful. Here are Sarah—her body is almost dead—and Abraham—his body is almost dead: *"As it is written, 'I have made you a father of many nations'"* (Rom. 4:17). "Now," says Abraham, "God has made me a father of many nations, and there is no hope of a son according to the natural law, no hope whatever." Here God says, *"I have made you a father of many nations,"* and yet Abraham has no son. During the past twenty years of waiting, conditions had grown more and more hopeless, and yet the promise was made.

85

Now, how long have you believed and still suffered from rheumatism? How long have you been waiting for the promise and it has not come? Did you need to wait? Look here! I want to tell you that all the people who are saved are blessed with faithful Abraham (Gal. 3:9). Abraham is the great substance of the whole keynote of Scripture; he is a man who dared for twenty-five years to believe God when everything got worse every day. Oh, it is lovely and perfect. I do not know anything in the Scriptures as marvelous, as far-reaching, and as full of the substance of living reality to change us if we will believe God. He will make us so different. This is a blessed incarnation of living faith that changes us and makes us know that God is, and that He is a rewarder of those who diligently seek Him (Heb. 11:6). God is a reality. God is true, and in Him there is no lie or shadow of turning (James 1:17). Oh, it is good! I do love to think about such truths as this.

Oh, beloved, there is not a subject in the whole Bible that makes my body aflame with passion after God and His righteousness as this. I see that He never fails. He wants the man to believe, and then the man will never fail. Oh, the loveliness of the character of God!

"A father of many nations." You talk about your infirmities—look at this! I have never felt I have had an infirmity since I understood this chapter. Oh, God, help me; I feel more like weeping than talking tonight. My cup runs over as I see the magnitude of this living God.

> *Therefore it is of faith that it might be according to grace, so that the promise might be sure*

> *to all the seed, not only to those who are of the law, but also to those who are of the faith of Abraham, who is the father of us all (as it is written, "I have made you a father of many nations") in the presence of Him whom he believed; God, who gives life to the dead and calls those things which do not exist as though they did; who, contrary to hope, in hope believed, so that he became the father of many nations, according to what was spoken, "So shall your descendants be."* (Rom. 4:16–18)

It is almost as if Abraham had said, "I won't look at my body. I won't look at my infirmities. I believe God will make the whole thing right." Some of us can say, "What does it matter if I have not heard for over twenty years? I believe my ears will be perfect." God is reality and wants us to know that if we will believe, it will be perfect. *"Who gives life to the dead and calls those things which do not exist as though they did."* There is no limitation of possibility.

Then God tested Abraham and Sarah still further than that. Oh, it is blessed to know you are tested. It is the greatest thing in the world to be tested. You never know what you are made of until you are tested. Some people say, "Oh, I don't know why my lot is such a heavy one," and God puts them into the fire again. He knows how to do it. I can tell you, He is a blessed God. There is no such thing as a groan when God gets hold of you. There is no such thing as lack to those who trust the Lord. When we really get in the will of God, He can make our enemies to be at peace with us (Prov. 16:7). It is wonderful.

I wonder if you really believe that God can quicken what is dead. I have seen it many times. The more there was no hope, Abraham believed in hope. Sometimes Satan will cloud your minds and interfere with your perception so that the obscure condition is brought right in between you and God, but God is able to change the whole position if you will let Him have a chance. Turn your back on every sense of unbelief, and believe God. There are some who would like to feel the presence of the touch of God; God will bring it to you. Now, I wish people could come to this place.

Abraham had a good time. The more he was squeezed, the more he rejoiced; and being not weak in faith, he did not consider his own body, which was weak when he was about a hundred years old, or the deadness of Sarah's womb. He did not waver through unbelief, but he was strong in faith, giving God the glory (Romans 4:19–20). God knows. He has a plan; He has a way. Do you dare trust Him? He knows.

I am here, saved by the power of God because of the promise that God made to Abraham: "As the countless sands upon the seashore and as the stars in multitude and glory, the seed of your son will be!" (See Genesis 22:16–18.) It is for us now. The Scripture says to us that the delaying of the promise and the testing of Abraham were the seed of all those in the world to come who would believe in God:

> *And being fully convinced that what He had promised He was also able to perform. And therefore "it was accounted to him for righteousness." Now it was not written for his sake alone that it was imputed to him, but also for us. It shall be imputed to us who believe in*

The Inheritance of Faith

*Him who raised up Jesus our Lord from the
dead.*   (Rom. 4:21–24)

The Promise Fulfilled

We have another place in the Scriptures, and I
want to touch upon it now. Isaac was born. And you
find that right in that house where Isaac was and
where Ishmael was, there was the seed of promise
and the seed of flesh. You find there is strife and
trouble right there, for Ishmael was teasing Isaac.
And you will find as sure as anything that there is
nothing that is going to hold you except the Isaac
life—the seed of Abraham. You will find that the
flesh life will always have to be cast out. And Sarah
said, *"Cast out* [Hagar] *and her son"* (Gen. 21:10). It
was very hard to do, but it had to be done. You may
say, "How hard!" Yes, but how long did it have to be?
It had to be until submission came. There will always be jealousy and strife in your hearts and lives
until flesh is destroyed, until Isaac controls and rules
in authority over the whole body. And when Isaac
power reigns over you, you will find that your whole
life is full of peace and joy.

Then the time came when this son Isaac grew up
to be a fine young man, perhaps twenty years of age—
we are not told—but then came another test. God
said to Abraham, "Take your son Isaac, and offer
him to Me upon the mount that I will show you."
(See Genesis 22:2.) Do you think that Abraham told
anybody about that? No, I am sure he didn't. Isaac
was near to his heart, and God said he had to offer
him on the altar, and there he was—Isaac, the heart
of his heart—and God said he was to be the seed of

89

all living. What did he have to do but believe that, just as miraculously as Isaac came into the world, God could raise him even if he were slain. Did he tell Sarah about the thing? No, I am certain he did not, or else he would not have gotten away with that boy. There would have been such a trial in the home. I believe he kept it to himself. When God tells you a secret, don't tell anyone else. God will possibly tell you to go and lay hands on some sick one. Go, do it, and don't tell anyone.

One thing I know is that Satan does not know my thoughts; he only knows what I let out of my mouth. Sometimes he suggests thoughts in order to get to know my thoughts, but I can see that God can captivate my thoughts in such a way that they may be entirely for Him. When God gets upon your hearts, you will see that every thought is captive, that everything is brought into obedience and is brought into a place where you are in dominion because Christ is enthroned in your life (2 Cor. 10:4–5). God reveals deep and special things to some people. Keep your counsel before God.

I see this: Abraham could offer Isaac. Now, tell me how. I believe that God wants me to tell you how so that you may know something about your trials. Some people think they are tried more than other people. If you knew the value of them, you would praise God for trials more than for anything. It is the trial that is used to purify you; it is the fiery furnace of affliction that God uses to get you in the place where He can use you. The person who has no trials and no difficulties is the person whom God does not dare allow Satan to touch because this person could not stand temptation. Nevertheless, Jesus will not allow any man to be tempted more than he is able to bear (1 Cor. 10:13).

The Scriptures are the strongest evidence of anything you can have. Before Abraham offered Isaac, he was tried, and God knew he could do it. And before God puts you through the furnace of afflictions, He knows you will go through. Not one single temptation comes to any man more than he is able to bear, and with the temptation, God is always there to help you through. Don't you see that was exactly the position in Abraham's case?

If you know you need the baptism of the Holy Spirit, and you know it is in the Scriptures, never rest until God gives it to you. If you know it is scriptural for you to be healed of every weakness, never rest until God makes the healing yours. If you know that the Scriptures teach holiness, purity, and divine likeness—overcoming under all conditions—never rest until you are an overcomer. If you know that men who have gone in and have seen the face of God, have had the vision revealed and have had all the Scriptures made to be life in their lives, never rest until you come to it. You say, "Do you have a Scripture to prove it?" Yes, the Scripture says, *"That you...may be able to comprehend with all the saints what is the width and length and depth and height; to know the love of Christ"* (Eph. 3:17–19).

Interpretation of Tongues

Oh, hallelujah! This blessed inheritance of the Spirit is come to profit withal, teaching you all things, and making you understand that the will of God comes not by observation, but holy men of old spoke and wrote as the Spirit gave them power and utterance. And so today the Holy Spirit must fill us with this same initiative of God.

We must live in the fire. We must hate sin; we must love righteousness. We must live with God, for He says we have to be blameless and harmless amid the crooked positions of the world. I look at you now, and I say God is able to confirm all I have been saying about trials and testings, which are the greatest blessings you can have. God wants to make sons everywhere like Jesus. Jesus was a type of the sonship that we have to strive to attain. I don't know how I feel when I am speaking about the loftiness of the character of Jesus, who was a firstfruit to make us pure and holy. And I see Jesus going about clothed with power. I likewise see every child of God clothed with power, and I see every detail. Jesus was just the firstfruit, and I know that is the pattern of God.

God has not given us a pattern that would be impossible to copy. Jesus hated sin, and this hatred is the greatest luxury we can have in our lives. If I have a hatred for sin, I have something that is worth millions. Oh, the blood of Jesus Christ, God's Son, cleanses us from all sin (1 John 1:7). I feel somehow that the hope of the church for the future is to be purified and made like Jesus: pure in heart, pure in thought. Then, when you lay your hands upon the sick, Satan has no power. When you command him to leave, he has to go. What a redemption! What a baptism! What an anointing! It is ecstasies of delight beyond all expression for the soul to live and move in Him who is our being.

8

Full! Full! Full!

nly believe! All things are possible; only believe! Praise God, He has made all things possible. There is liberty for everyone, whatever the trouble. Our Lord Jesus says, *"Only believe"* (Mark 5:36). He has obtained complete victory over every difficulty, over every power of evil, over every depravity. Every sin is covered by Calvary.

Who are of the tribe of Abraham? All who believe in Jesus Christ are the seed of faith, Abraham's seed. If we dare come believing, God will heal; God will restore and will lift the burden and will wake us up to real, overcoming faith. Look up; take courage! Jesus has shaken the foundations of death and darkness. He fights for you, and there is none like Him. He is the great I Am. His name is above every name. As we believe, we are lifted into a place of rest, a place of conformity to Him. He says to us as He did to Abraham, *"I will bless you...and you shall be a blessing"* (Gen. 12:2). He says to us as He did to His people of old, *"With lovingkindness I have drawn you"* (Jer. 31:3). Hallelujah! "He'll never forget to keep me, He'll never forget to keep me; my Father has many dear children, but He'll never forget to keep me." Believe it. He will never forget.

Live by the Power of the Spirit

In the sixth chapter of Acts, we read of the appointment of seven deacons. The disciples desired to give themselves wholly to prayer and to the ministry of the Word, and they said to the brothers, *"Seek out from among you seven men of good reputation, full of the Holy Spirit and wisdom, whom we may appoint over this business"* (Acts 6:3). And they chose Stephen, *"a man full of faith and the Holy Spirit"* (v. 5), and six others. We read that Stephen, full of faith and power, did great wonders and miracles among the people (v. 8), and his opponents were not able to resist the wisdom and the spirit by which he spoke. When his opponents brought him before the Sanhedrin, all who sat in the council looked steadfastly on him, and they *"saw his face as the face of an angel"* (v. 15).

I see many remarkable things in the life of Stephen. One thing moves me, and that is the truth that I must live by the power of the Spirit at all costs. God wants us to be like Stephen: full of faith and full of the Holy Spirit (v. 5). You can never be the same again after you have received this wonderful baptism in the Holy Spirit. It is important that we should be full of wisdom and faith day by day and full of the Holy Spirit, acting by the power of the Holy Spirit. God has set us here in the last days, these days of apostasy, and wants us to be burning and shining lights in the midst of an indecent generation. God is longing for us to come into such a fruitful position as the sons of God, with the marks of heaven upon us, and His divinity bursting through our humanity, that He can express Himself through our lips of clay. He can take clay lips and weak humanity and make an oracle for Himself of such things. He can take frail human nature and by His divine power make our bodies suitable to be His holy temple, washing our hearts whiter than snow.

Our Lord Jesus says, *"All authority has been given to Me in heaven and on earth"* (Matt. 28:18). He longs that we would be filled with faith and with the Holy Spirit, and He declares to us, *"He who believes in Me, the works that I do he will do also; and greater works than these he will do, because I go to My Father"* (John 14:12). He has gone to the Father. He is in the place of power, and He exercises His power not only in heaven but also on earth, for He has all power on earth as well as in heaven. Hallelujah! What an open door to us if we will only believe Him!

The disciples were men after our standard as far as the flesh goes. God sent them forth, joined to the Lord and identified with Him. How diverse Peter, John, and Thomas were! Impulsive Peter was always ready to go forth without a stop. John, the beloved, leaned on the Master's breast, and how different that was! Thomas had a hard nature and defiant spirit: *"Unless I...put my finger into the print of the nails, and put my hand into His side, I will not believe"* (John 20:25). What strange flesh! How peculiar they were! But the Master could mold them. There was no touch like His.

Under His touch, even stony-hearted Thomas believed. Oh, my God, how You have had to manage some of us! Have we not been strange and very peculiar? But, when God's hand comes upon us, He can speak to us in such a way; He can give us a word or a look, and we are broken. Has He spoken to you? I thank God for His speaking. Behind all of His dealings, we see the love of God for us. It is not what we are that counts, but what we can be as He disciplines, chastens, and transforms us by His all-skillful hands. He sees our bitter tears and our weeping night after night. There is none like Him. He knows; He forgives. We cannot forgive ourselves; we oftentimes would give the world to forget, but we cannot. The devil won't let us forget. But God has forgiven and forgotten. Do you believe self or the devil or God? Which are you going to believe? Believe God. I know the past is under the blood and that God has forgiven and forgotten, for when He forgives, He forgets. Praise the Lord! Hallelujah! We are baptized to believe and to receive.

Full of Faith and Power

In making provision for the serving of tables and the daily distribution, the disciples knew who were baptized with the Holy Spirit. In the early days of the church, all who did the work had to be men full of the Holy Spirit. I am hungry that I may be more full, that God may choose me for His service. And I know that the greatest qualification is to be filled with the Spirit. The Holy Spirit has the divine commission from heaven to impart revelation to every son of God concerning the Lord Jesus, to unfold to us the gifts and the fruit of the Spirit. He will take of the things of Christ and show them to us.

Full! Full! Full!

Stephen was a man full of faith and the Holy Spirit. God declares it. God so manifested Himself in Stephen's body that he became an epistle of truth, known and read by all. He was full of faith! Such men never talk doubtfully. You never hear them say, "I wish it could be so," or "If it is God's will." They have no *if*s; they know. You never hear them say, "Well, it is not always so." They say, "It is sure to be." They laugh at impossibilities and cry, "It will be done!" A man full of faith hopes against hope. He shouts while the walls are up, and they come down while he shouts. God has this faith for us in Christ. We must be careful that no unbelief and no wavering are found in us.

"Stephen, full of faith and power, did great wonders and signs among the people" (Acts 6:8). The Holy Spirit could do mighty things through him because he believed God, and God is with the man who dares to believe His Word. All things were possible because of the Holy Spirit's position in Stephen's body. He was full of the Holy Spirit, so God could fulfill His purposes through him. When a child of God is filled with the Holy Spirit, the Spirit *"makes intercession for the saints according to the will of God"* (Rom. 8:27). He fills us with longings and desires until we are in a place of fervency like a glowing fire. We do not know what to do. When we are in this place, the Holy Spirit begins to work. When the Holy Spirit has liberty in the body, He conveys all utterance into the presence of God according to the will of God. Such prayers are always heard. Such praying is always answered; it is never bare of result. When we are praying in the Holy Spirit, faith is evident, and as a result the power of God can be manifested in our midst.

When some of the various synagogues arose to dispute with Stephen, they were not able to resist the wisdom and the Spirit by which he spoke. When we are filled with the Holy Spirit, we will have wisdom.

The Power of the Spirit

Praise God! One night I was entrusted with a meeting, and I was guarding my position before God. I wanted approval from the Lord. I saw that God wants men full of the Holy Spirit, with divine ability, filled with life, a flaming fire. In the meeting a young man stood up. He was a pitiful object with a face full of sorrow. I said, "What is it, young man?"

He said he was unable to work, and he could scarcely walk. He said, "I am so helpless. I have consumption and a weak heart, and my body is full of pain."

I said, "I will pray for you." I said to the people, "As I pray for this young man, you look at his face and see it change."

As I prayed, his face changed. I said to him, "Go out, run a mile, and come back to the meeting."

He came back and said, "I can now breathe freely."

The meetings were continuing, and I missed him. After a few days I saw him again in a meeting. I said, "Young man, tell the people what God has done for you."

"Oh," he said, "I have been able to work and make money."

Praise God, this wonderful stream of salvation never runs dry. You can take a drink; it is close to you. It is a river that is running deep, and there is plenty for all.

In a meeting a man rose and said, "Will you touch me? I am in a terrible situation. I have a family of children, and because of an accident in the pit, I have had no work for two years. I cannot open my hands." I was full of sorrow for this poor man, and something happened that had never happened before. We are in the infancy of this wonderful outpouring of the Holy Spirit, and there is so much more for us. I put out my hand, and before my hands reached his, he was loosed and made perfectly free.

I see that Stephen, full of faith and of power, did great wonders and miracles among the people. This same Holy Spirit filling is for us, and right things will be accomplished if we are filled with His Spirit. God will grant it. He declares that the desires of the righteous will be granted (Prov. 10:24). Stephen was an ordinary man made extraordinary in God. We may be very ordinary, but God wants to make us extraordinary in the Holy Spirit. God is ready to touch and transform you right now.

Once a woman rose in the meeting asking for prayer. I prayed for her, and she was healed. She cried out, "It is a miracle! It is a miracle! It is a miracle!" That is what God wants to do for us all the time. As surely as we get free in the Holy Spirit, something will happen. Let us pursue the best things, and let God have His right-of-way.

All who sat in the council looked steadfastly on Stephen and saw his face as the face of an angel (Acts 6:15). It was worth being filled with the Holy Spirit for that. The Spirit is breaking through. There is a touch of the Spirit in which the light of God will truly radiate from our faces.

The seventh chapter of Acts is the profound prophetic utterance that the Spirit spoke through this holy man. The Word of God flowed through the lips of Stephen in the form of divine prophecy so that those who heard these things were cut to the heart. But he, being full of the Holy Spirit, looked up steadfastly into heaven and saw the glory of God and Jesus standing on the right hand of God, and he said, *"Look! I see the heavens opened and the Son of Man standing at the right hand of God!"* (Acts 7:56). Stephen was full of the Holy Spirit right to the end. He saw Jesus standing. In another part we read of Him seated at the right hand of God. That is His place of authority. But here we see that He arose. He was so keenly interested in that martyr Stephen. May the Lord open our eyes to see Him and to know that He is deeply interested in all that concerns us. He is touched with the feeling of our infirmities.

All things are naked and open to the eyes of Him with whom we are connected (Heb. 4:13). He knows about that asthma. He knows about that rheumatism. He knows about that pain in the back, head, or feet. He wants to loose every captive and to set you free just as He has set me free. I hardly know that I have a body today. I am free from every human ailment, absolutely free. Christ has redeemed us. He has power over all the power of the enemy and has worked out our great victory. Will you have it? It is yours; it is a perfect redemption.

And they stoned Stephen, who called upon God: *"'Lord Jesus, receive my spirit.' Then he knelt down and cried out with a loud voice, 'Lord, do not charge them with this sin.' And when he had said this, he fell asleep"* (Acts 7:59–60). Stephen was not only filled with faith, but he was also filled with love as he prayed just as his Master had prayed, *"Father, forgive them"* (Luke 23:34).

It is God's thought to make us a new creation, with all the old things passed away and all things within us truly of God; to bring in a new, divine order, a perfect love and an unlimited faith. Will you have it? Redemption is free. Arise in the activity of faith, and God will heal you as you rise. Only believe, and receive in faith. Stephen, full of faith and of the Holy Spirit, did great signs and wonders (Acts 6:8). May God bless to us this passage and fill us full of His Holy Spirit and through the power of the Holy Spirit reveal Christ in us more and more.

The Spirit of God will always reveal the Lord Jesus Christ. Serve Him; love Him; be filled with Him. It is lovely to hear Him as He makes Himself known to us. He is the same yesterday, today, and forever (Heb. 13:8). He is willing to fill us with the Holy Spirit and faith just as He filled Stephen.

9

Have Faith in God

*For assuredly, I say to you, whoever says to this
mountain, "Be removed and be cast into the sea," and
does not doubt in his heart, but believes that those
things he says will be done, he will have
whatever he says. Therefore I say to you, whatever
things you ask when you pray, believe that you receive
them, and you will have them.*
—Mark 11:23–24

hese are days when we need to have our faith
strengthened, when we need to know God. God
has designed that the just will live by faith
(Rom. 1:17), no matter how he may be fettered. I
know that God's Word is sufficient. One word from
Him can change a nation. His Word is *"from everlasting to everlasting"* (Ps. 90:2). It is through the en-
trance of this everlasting Word, this incorruptible
seed, that we are born again and come into this wonderful salvation. *"Man shall not live by bread alone,
but by every word that proceeds from the mouth of
God"* (Matt. 4:4). This is the food of faith. *"Faith
comes by hearing, and hearing by the word of God"*
(Rom. 10:17).

God's Word Is Sure

Everywhere men are trying to discredit the Bible and take from it all that is miraculous in it. One preacher says, "Well, you know, Jesus arranged beforehand to have that colt tied where it was and for the men to say just what they did." (See Matthew 21:2–3.) I tell you, God can arrange everything. He can plan for you, and when He plans for you, all is peace. All things are possible if you will believe.

Another preacher says, "It was an easy thing for Jesus to feed the people with five loaves. The loaves were so big in those days that it was a simple matter to cut them into a thousand pieces each." (See John 6:5–13.) But he forgets that one little boy brought those five loaves all the way in his lunch basket. There is nothing impossible with God. All the impossibility is with us when we measure God by the limitations of our unbelief.

Reaching Out in Faith

We have a wonderful God, a God whose ways are past finding out and whose grace and power are limitless. I was in Belfast one day and saw one of the brothers of the assembly. He said to me, "Wigglesworth, I am troubled. I have had a good deal of sorrow during the past five months. I had a woman in my assembly who could always pray the blessing of heaven down on our meetings. She is an old woman, but her presence is always an inspiration. But five months ago she fell and broke her leg. The doctors put her into a plaster cast, and after five months they broke the cast. But the bones were not properly set, and so she fell and broke the leg again."

He took me to her house, and there was a woman lying in a bed on the right-hand side of the room. I said to her, "Well, what about it now?"

She said, "They have sent me home incurable. The doctors say that I am so old that my bones won't knit. There is no nutriment in my bones. They could not do anything for me, and they say I will have to lie in bed for the rest of my life."

I said to her, "Can you believe God?"

She replied, "Yes, ever since I heard that you had come to Belfast my faith has been quickened. If you will pray, I will believe. I know there is no power on earth that can make the bones of my leg knit, but I know there is nothing impossible with God."

I said, "Do you believe He will meet you now?"

She answered, "I do."

It is grand to see people believe God. God knew all about this leg and that it was broken in two places. I said to the woman, "When I pray, something will happen."

Her husband was sitting there; he had been in his chair for four years and could not walk a step. He called out, "I don't believe. I won't believe. You will never get me to believe."

I said, "All right," and laid my hands on his wife in the name of the Lord Jesus.

The moment hands were laid upon her, she cried out, "I'm healed."

I said, "I'm not going to assist you to rise. God will do it all." She arose and walked up and down the room, praising God.

The old man was amazed at what had happened to his wife, and he cried out, "Make me walk, make me walk."

I said to him, "You old sinner, repent."

He cried out, "Lord, You know I believe."

I don't think he meant what he said; anyhow the Lord was full of compassion. If He marked our sins, where would any of us be? If we will meet the conditions, God will always meet us if we believe all things are possible.

I laid my hands on him, and the power went right through the old man's body. For the first time in four years, those legs received power to carry his body. He walked up and down and in and out of the room. He said, "Oh, what great things God has done for us tonight!"

"Whatever things you ask when you pray, believe that you receive them, and you will have them." Desire God, and you will have desires from God. He will meet you on the line of those desires when you reach out in simple faith.

A man came to me in one of my meetings who had seen other people healed and wanted to be healed, too. He explained that his arm had been set in a certain position for many years, and he could not move it. "Got any faith?" I asked.

He said that he had a lot of faith. After prayer he was able to swing his arm round and round. But he was not satisfied and complained, "I feel a little bit of trouble just there," pointing to a certain place.

I said, "Do you know what the trouble is with you?"

He answered, "No."

I said, "Imperfect faith." *"Whatever things you ask when you pray, believe that you receive them, and you will have them."*

Did you believe before you were saved? So many people want to be saved, but they want to feel saved first. There never was a man who felt saved before he believed. God's plan is always the following: if you will believe, you will see the glory of God (John 11:40). I believe God wants to bring us all to a definite place of unswerving faith and confidence in Himself.

In our text from Mark, Jesus uses the illustration of a mountain. Why does He say a mountain? If faith can remove a mountain, it can remove anything. The plan of God is so marvelous that if you will only believe, all things are possible (Mark 9:23).

Love Has No Doubts

There is one special phrase from our text to which I want to call your attention: *"And does not doubt in his heart."* The heart is the mainspring. Imagine a young man and a young woman. They have fallen in love at first sight. In a short while there is a deep affection and a strong heart love, the one toward the other. What is a heart of love? It is a heart of faith. Faith and love are kin. In the measure that the young man and the young woman love one another, they are true. One may go to the North and the other to the South, but because of their love, they will be true to one another.

It is the same when there is a deep love in the heart toward the Lord Jesus Christ. In this new life into which God has brought us, Paul told us that we have become dead to the law by the body of Christ, so that we should be married to another, even to Him who is raised from the dead (Rom. 7:4). God brings us into a place of perfect love and perfect faith. A man who is born of God is brought into an inward affection, a loyalty to the Lord Jesus that shrinks from anything impure. You see the purity of a man and woman when there is a deep natural affection between them; they disdain the very thought of either of them being untrue. In the same way, in the measure that a man has faith in Jesus, he is pure. He who believes that Jesus is the Christ overcomes the world (1 John 5:5). It is a faith that works by love (Gal. 5:6).

Just as we have heart fellowship with our Lord, our faith cannot be daunted. We cannot doubt in our hearts. As we go on with God, there comes a wonderful association, an impartation of His very life and nature within. As we read His Word and believe the promises that He has so graciously given to us, we are made partakers of His very essence and life. The Lord is made a Bridegroom to us, and we are His bride. His words to us are spirit and life, transforming us and changing us, expelling what is natural and bringing in what is divine.

It is impossible to comprehend the love of God as we think along natural lines. We must have the revelation from the Spirit of God. God gives liberally. He who asks, receives (Matt. 7:8). God is willing to bestow on us all things that pertain to life and godliness (2 Pet. 1:3). Oh, it was the love of God that brought Jesus, and it is this same love that helps you and me to believe. God will be your strength in every weakness. You who need His touch, remember that He loves you. If you are wretched, helpless, or sick, look to the God of all grace, whose very essence is love, who delights to give liberally all the inheritance of life and strength and power that you are in need of.

Be Cleansed Today

When I was in Switzerland, the Lord was graciously working and healing many of the people. I was staying with Brother Reuss of Goldiwil, and two policemen were sent to arrest me. The charge was that I was healing the people without a license. Mr. Reuss said to them, "I am sorry that he is not here just now; he is holding a meeting about two miles away, but before you arrest him I would like to show you something."

Brother Reuss took these two policemen down to one of the lower parts of that district, to a house with which they were familiar, for they had often gone to that place to arrest a certain woman who was constantly an inmate of the prison because of continually being engaged in drunken brawls. He took them to this woman and said to them, "This is one of the many cases of blessing that have come through the ministry of the man you have come to arrest. This woman came to our meeting in a drunken condition. Her body was broken, for she was ruptured in two places. While she was drunk, the evangelist laid his hands on her and asked God to heal her and deliver her."

The woman joined in, "Yes, and God saved me, and I have not tasted a drop of liquor since."

The policemen had a warrant for my arrest, but they said with disgust, "Let the doctors do this kind of thing." They turned and went away, and that was the last we heard of them.

We have a Jesus who heals the brokenhearted, who lets the captives go free, who saves the very worst. Do you dare spurn this glorious Gospel of God for spirit, soul, and body? Do you dare spurn this grace? I realize that this full Gospel has in great measure been hidden, this Gospel that brings liberty, this Gospel that brings souls out of bondage, this Gospel that brings perfect health to the body, this Gospel of entire salvation. Listen again to the words of Him who left the glory to bring us this great salvation: *"Assuredly, I say to you, whoever says to this mountain, 'Be removed'...he will have whatever he says."* Whatever!

I realize that God can never bless us when we are being hard-hearted, critical, or unforgiving. These things will hinder faith quicker than anything. I remember being at a meeting where there were some people waiting for the baptism and seeking for cleansing, for the moment a person is cleansed the Spirit will fall. There was one man with red eyes who was weeping bitterly. He said to me, "I will have to leave. It is no good my staying unless I change things. I have written a letter to my brother-in-law and filled it with hard words, and this thing must first be straightened out." He went home and told his wife, "I'm going to write a letter to your brother and ask him to forgive me for writing to him the way I did."

"You fool!" she said.

"Never mind," he replied, "this thing is between God and me, and it has got to be cleared away." He wrote the letter and came again, and immediately God filled him with the Spirit.

Have Faith in God

I believe there are a great many people who want to be healed, but they are harboring things in their hearts that are like a blight. Let these things go. Forgive, and the Lord will forgive you. There are many good people, people who mean well, but they have no power to do anything for God. There is just some little thing that came in their hearts years ago, and their faith has been paralyzed ever since. Bring everything to the light. God will sweep it all away if you will let Him. Let the precious blood of Christ cleanse you from all sin. If you will only believe, God will meet you and bring into your lives the sunshine of His love.

10

The Hour Is Come

es, I believe! I hope that our hearts and minds might come to that place of understanding where we realize that it is possible for God to take all our human weaknesses and failures and transform us by His mighty power into a new creation if we *"only believe"* (Mark 5:36). What an inspiration it is to give God the supreme place in our lives! When we do, He will so fill us with the Holy Spirit that the government will rest upon His shoulders. (See Isaiah 9:6.) I hope that we will believe and come into the holy realm of the knowledge of what it means to yield our all to God. Just think of what would happen if we only dared to believe God! We need a faith that leaps into the will of God and says, "Amen!"

The Lord's Supper

There is no service so wonderful to me as the service of partaking in the Lord's Supper, the Holy Communion. The Scriptures say, *"This do, as often as you* [do] *it, in remembrance of Me"* (1 Cor. 11:25);

113

you do it in remembrance of Him. I am sure that every person in this place has a great desire to do something for Jesus, and what He wants to do for us is to keep in remembrance of the cross, the grave, the Resurrection, and the Ascension, for the memory of these four events will always bring you into a place of great blessing. You do not need, however, to continually live on the cross, or even in remembrance of the cross, but what you need to remember about the cross is, *"It is finished"* (John 19:30). You do not need to live in the grave, but only keep in remembrance that *"He is risen"* (Matt. 28:6) out of the grave and that we are to be seated *"with Him in glory"* (Col. 3:4). The institution of the Holy Communion is one of those settings in Scripture, a time in the history of our Lord Jesus Christ when the mystery of the glories of Christ was being unveiled. As the Master walked on this earth, the multitudes would gather with eagerness and longing in their hearts to hear the words that dropped from His gracious lips. But there were also those who had missed the vision. They saw the Christ, heard His words, but those wonderful words were like idle tales to them.

When we miss the vision and do not come into the fullness of the ministry of the Spirit, there is a cause. Beloved, there is a deadness in us that must have the resurrection touch. Today we have the unveiled truth, for the dispensation of the Holy Spirit has come to unfold the fullness of redemption, that we might be clothed with power, and what brings us into the state where God can pour upon us His blessing is a broken spirit and a contrite heart (Ps. 51:17). We need to examine ourselves this morning to see what state we are in, whether we are just religious or whether are truly in Christ.

The human spirit, when perfectly united with the Holy Spirit, has but one place, and that is death, death, and deeper death. In this place, the human spirit will cease to desire to have its own way, and instead of "My will," the cry of the heart will be, "May Your will, O Lord, be done in me."

God's Word Is True

And He sent Peter and John, saying, "Go and prepare the Passover for us, that we may eat." So they said to Him, "Where do You want us to prepare?" And He said to them, "Behold, when you have entered the city, a man will meet you carrying a pitcher of water; follow him into the house which he enters. Then you shall say to the master of the house, 'The Teacher says to you, "Where is the guest room where I may eat the Passover with My disciples?"' Then he will show you a large, furnished upper room; there make ready." (Luke 22:8–12)

It is one thing to handle the Word of God, but it is another thing to believe what God says. The great aim of the Spirit's power within us is to so bring us in line with His perfect will that we will unhesitatingly believe the Scriptures, daring to accept them as the authentic, divine principle of God. When we do, we will find our feet so firmly fixed upon the plan of redemption that it will not matter where our trials or other things come from, because our whole natures will be so enlarged that we will no longer focus on ourselves but will say, *"Lord, what do You want me to do?"* (Acts 9:6).

Every believer should be a living epistle of the Word, one who is read and known by all men (2 Cor. 3:2). Your very presence should bring such a witness of the Spirit that everyone with whom you come in contact would know that you are a sent one, a light in the world, a manifestation of the Christ, and last of all, a biblical Christian.

Those disciples had to learn that whatever Jesus said must come to pass. Jesus said, very slowly and thoughtfully I believe,

> *Behold, when you have entered the city, a man will meet you carrying a pitcher of water; follow him into the house which he enters. Then you shall say to the master of the house, "The Teacher says to you, 'Where is the guest room where I may eat the Passover with My disciples?'"* (Luke 22:10–11)

That is the way that Jesus taught them. Beloved, let me say this, there was no person in Palestine who had ever seen a man bearing a pitcher of water. It is an unknown thing. Therefore, we find Jesus beginning with a prophecy that brought that inward knowledge to them that what He said must come to pass. This is the secret of the Master's life: prophecy that never failed. There is no power that can change the Word of God. Jesus was working out this great thought in the hearts of His disciples, that they might know that it would come to pass. After Jesus had given that wonderful command to Peter and John, those disciples were walking into the city, no doubt in deep meditation, when suddenly they cried out in amazement, "Look! There he is! Just as the Master has said."

When I was in Jerusalem, I was preaching on Mount Olivet. As I looked down to my right I saw where the two ways met, where the donkey was tied. I could see the Dead Sea, and all the time I was preaching I saw at least 150 women going down with pitchers and then carrying them back on their heads, full of water, but I did not see one man. However, Jesus said that it had to be a man, and so it was, for no one could change His word.

Some have said to me that He had it all arranged for a man to carry a pitcher of water. I want to tell you that God does not have to arrange with mortals to carry out His plans. God has the power to hear the cry of some poor needy child of His who may be suffering in England, Africa, China, or anywhere else, saying, "O God, You know my need." At the same time in New York, Germany, California, or some other place, there is a disciple of His on his knees, and the Lord will say to him, "Send help to that brother or sister, and do not delay it." And so the help comes. He did not need to get a man to help Him out by carrying a pitcher of water. He works according to His Word, and Jesus said a man would carry water.

What did those disciples do as they saw the man? Did they go forward to meet him? No, they waited for the man, and when he came up, they probably walked alongside of him without a word until he was about to enter the house. Then I can hear one saying to him, "Please, sir, the Master wants the guest chamber!" "The guest chamber?

Why, I was preparing it all day yesterday but did not know whom it was for." With man things are impossible, but God is the unfolder of the mysteries of life and holds the universe in the hollow of His hand. What we need to know now is that *"the LORD thy God in the midst of thee is mighty"* (Zeph. 3:17 KJV), and He works according to His Word.

The Word of God Lives Today

When the hour had come, He sat down, and the twelve apostles with Him. Then He said to them, "With fervent desire I have desired to eat this Passover with you before I suffer; for I say to you, I will no longer eat of it until it is fulfilled in the kingdom of God." Then He took the cup, and gave thanks, and said, "Take this and divide it among yourselves; for I say to you, I will not drink of the fruit of the vine until the kingdom of God comes." And He took bread, gave thanks and broke it, and gave it to them, saying, "This is My body which is given for you; do this in remembrance of Me."

(Luke 22:14–19)

It takes the Master to bring the Word home to our hearts. His was a ministry that brought a new vision to mankind, for *"no man ever spoke like this Man!"* (John 7:46). How I love to hear Him preach! How He says things! I have watched Him as He trod this earth. Enter into the Scriptures, and watch the Lord. Follow Him; take notice of His counsel, and you will have a story of wonders. The Book speaks today. It is life, and looms up full of glory. It reflects and unfolds with a new creative power.

The Hour Is Come

The words of Jesus are life—never think they are less. If you believe them, you will feel quickened. The Word is powerful; it is full of faith. The Word of God is vital. Listen: *"The word...did not profit them, not being mixed with faith in those who heard it"* (Heb. 4:2). There has to be hearing in order to have faith. Faith is established and made manifest as we hear the Word. Beloved, read the Word of God in quietude, and read it out loud so that you can hear it, for *"he who hears My word"* (John 5:24), to him it gives life.

Listen: *"With fervent desire"* (Luke 22:15); *"the hour has come"* (Mark 14:41). He speaks. From the beginning of time, there has never been an hour like this. These words were among the greatest that He ever spoke: *"The hour has come."* What an hour, for the end of time had come. "What?" you ask. Yes, I repeat it, for the redemption of the cross, the shedding of the blood, had brought in a new hour.

Time was finished and eternity had begun for every soul that was covered with the blood. Until that hour all people lived only to die, but the moment the sacrifice was made, it was not the end but only the beginning. Time was finished, and eternity had begun. The soul, covered with the blood, has moved from a natural to an eternal union with the Lord. Then the commandment, "You shall not," which had so worried the people and brought them into such dissatisfaction because they could not keep the Law, was changed into a new commandment. It was no more, "You shall not," but, *"I delight to do Your will, O my God"* (Ps. 40:8). *"In Adam all die"* (1 Cor. 15:22), but now *"the hour has come"* (Mark 14:41). *"In Christ all shall be made alive"* (1 Cor. 15:22). Instead of death will be the fullness of life divine.

"I have a desire to eat this Passover with you before I suffer. I know that within a few moments the judgment hall awaits me." Do you think that I could be in Jerusalem and not want to pass through the gate that He went through? Do you think that I could be in Jerusalem and not want to pass over the Brook Kidron? Could you imagine me being in Jerusalem and not wanting to go into the Garden or view the tomb where His body was laid? I knelt down at that holy place, for I felt that I must commune with my Lord there.

While I was in Jerusalem, I preached many weeks outside the Damascus Gate, and God mightily blessed my ministry. It is wonderful to be in the place where God can use you. As I was leaving Jerusalem, some Jews who had heard me preach wanted to travel with me, and they wanted to stay at the same hotel where I was staying. When we were sitting around the table eating, they said, "What we cannot understand is that when you preach we feel such power. You move us. There is something about it; we cannot help but feel that you have something different from what we have been used to hearing. Why is it?"

I replied that it was because I preached Jesus in the power of the Holy Spirit, for He was the Messiah, and He causes a child of His to so live in the reality of a clear knowledge of Himself that others know and feel His power. It is this knowledge that the church today is very much in need of.

Do not be satisfied with anything less than the knowledge of a real change in your nature, the knowledge of the indwelling presence and power of the Holy Spirit. Do not be satisfied with a life that is not wholly swallowed up in God.

There are many books written on the Word, and we love clear, definite teaching on it. But go to the Book, and listen to what the Master says. You will lay a sure foundation that cannot be moved, for we are born again by the incorruptible Word of God (1 Pet. 1:23). We need that simplicity, that rest of faith, that brings us to the place where we are steadfast and immovable. How wonderful the living Word of God is!

Can you not see that the Master was so interested in you that He would despise the shame and despise the cross? The judgment hall was nothing to Him; all the rebukes and scorn could not take from Him the joy of saving you and me. It was that joy that caused Him to say, "I count nothing too vile for Wigglesworth; I count nothing too vile for Brown; for my soul is on the wing to save the world!" How beautiful this is! How it should thrill us! He knew that death was represented in that sacred cup, and yet He joyfully said, *"With fervent desire I have desired to eat this Passover with you before I suffer"* (Luke 22:15). Take the bread, drink of the cup, and as often as you take it, remember (1 Cor. 11:24–25). In other words, take the memory of what it means home with you; think on it, and analyze its meaning.

Jesus brought in a new creation by the words of His ministry. *"Among those born of women there has not risen one greater than John the Baptist; but he who is least in the kingdom of heaven is greater than he"* (Matt. 11:11). He said that *"the kingdom of God is within you"* (Luke 17:21) and that He would *"no longer drink of the fruit of the vine until that day when I drink it new in the kingdom of God"* (Mark 14:25). He also said that every person who has the

121

new nature, the new birth, has the kingdom of God within him. If you believe God's Word, it will make you so live that the kingdom of God will always be increasing; and the whole creation of the kingdom of God will be crying, "Come, Lord Jesus, come!" (See Revelation 22:20), and He will come.

As we come to the time of the breaking of bread, the thought should be, "How should I partake of it?" If before His death He could take it and say, *"With fervent desire I have desired to eat this Passover with you before I suffer"* (Luke 22:15), we should be able to say, "Lord, I desire to eat it to please You, for I want my whole life to be for You!" What grace there is! As the stream of the new life begins to flow through your being, allow yourself to be immersed and carried on with an ever increasing flow until your life becomes a ceaseless flow of the river of life, and then it will be *"No longer I...but Christ...in me"* (Gal. 2:20).

Get ready for the breaking of bread, and in doing so, remember. Get ready for partaking of the wine, and in doing so, remember Him.

11

Filled with God's Fullness

To those who have obtained like precious faith with
us by the righteousness of our God and
Savior Jesus Christ.
—2 Peter 1:1

od has always had a person whom He could
illuminate and enlarge until there was nothing hindering the power of God flowing out to
a world in need. This *"like...faith"* is the gift God is
willing to give us in order, if need be, that we may
subdue kingdoms, work righteousness, and stop the
mouths of lions (Heb. 11:33). It is the ability to triumph under all circumstances because our helper is
Almighty God, and He is always strong and faithful.
The faithful—living in the divine order of victory—
always have a good report because God has taken
His place in them. The divine Author brings to our
minds "Thus says the Lord" every time. If any man
should speak, let him speak as an oracle of God,
having the Word of God as the standard for all need.

This *"like...faith"* is the same faith that Abraham had. It counts the things that are not as though

they are, and it believes that what God has is the essence of the substance of the power of eternal life.

Jesus is the Word, and if you have the Word, you have faith: *"like...faith."* There is no way into the power and deep things of God without a broken spirit. We should be erasing from ourselves and allowing God to take the reins and rule. Faith in God and power with God lie in the knowledge of the Word of God. We are no better than our faith. *"For whatever is born of God overcomes the world. And this is the victory that has overcome the world; our faith"* (1 John 5:4). If you believe in Him, you are purified, for He is pure. You are strengthened, for He is strong. You are made whole, because He is whole.

The Living Principle

You may receive all His fullness because of the revelation of Him. This *"like...faith"* is imparted in all the principles of the Word of God. Faith is the living principle of the Word of God. If we are led by God's Spirit, we will definitely be led into the deep things of God and His truth. The revelation of Him will be so clear that we will live by His life.

Now, beloved, I cannot understand God except by His Word, not by impressions, feelings, or sentiment. If I am going to know God, I am going to know Him by His Word. There is a divine act for every man who is born of God when God comes in, working in him a personality of Himself—Christ formed in us.

God is almighty; there is no limitation. And His purpose is to bring many souls to glory. He speaks about His divine power, which has given us all things that pertain to life and godliness through the knowledge of Him (2 Pet. 1:3). God's Word is multiplication—yesterday, today, and forever the same.

God wants to give a great multiplication in the knowledge of Himself. Then faith will be used, and we will know the wonderful flow of the peace of God. If we open ourselves to God, God will flow through us.

If we know God hears us when we pray, we know we have the petition we have desired.

The Living Word

God's Word is:

Supernatural in origin.
Eternal in duration.
Inexpressible in valor.
Infinite in scope.
Regenerative in power.
Infallible in authority.
Universal in application.
Inspired in totality.

Thus, we should:

Read it through.
Write it down.
Pray it in.
Work it out.
Pass it on.

The Word of God changes a man until he becomes an epistle of God. The Word transforms the mind, changes the character from grace to grace, and gives us an inheritance in the Spirit, until we are conformed—God coming in, dwelling in us, walking in us, talking through us, and eating with us. There is no God like our God. I believe in the Holy Spirit.

God is love. *"He who abides in love abides in God"* (1 John 4:16). God wants to take ordinary men and bring them out into extraordinary conditions.

God has room for the thirsty man who is crying out for more of Himself.

It is not what we are, but it is what God wants us to be.

Blessed are the poor in spirit, for Christ is the kingdom of heaven (Matt. 5:3). Beloved, let us rededicate ourselves afresh to God! Every new revelation means a new dedication.

Let us seek His face, and let us take away from this meeting the desire of our hearts. For God has promised to fulfill, fill full, the desire of those who fear Him.

> Like, like faith,
> Like fulfillment. Amen.

12

A Living Faith

Praise God! There is something that brings us all to this meeting. What will it be like when we get rid of this body of flesh and when Jesus is the light of the city of God? Nevertheless, God means for us to put on the whole armor of God (Eph. 6:11) while we are here. He wants us to be covered with the covering of His Spirit and to grow in grace and the knowledge of God.

Oh, what God has laid up for us, and what we may receive through the name of Jesus! Oh, the value of the name, the power of the name; the very name of Jesus brings help from heaven, and the very name of Jesus can bind evil powers and *"subdue all things to Himself"* (Phil 3:21). Thank God for victory through our Lord Jesus Christ.

The Author of Our Faith

For the sake of saving us, He endured the cross, despising the shame (Heb. 12:2). How beautiful it is to say with our whole will, "I will be obedient unto God." Oh, He is lovely; He is beautiful. I do not remember Him ever denying me anything when I have come to Him; He has never turned me away empty. He is such a wonderful Savior, such a Friend that we can depend upon with assurance and rest and complete confidence. He can roll away every burden.

Think of Him as the exhaustless Savior, the everlasting Friend, One who knows all things, One who is able to help and deliver us. When we have such a Source as this, we can stretch out our hands and take all that we need from Him.

Let's turn to the eleventh chapter of Mark's gospel.

> *And Jesus went into Jerusalem and into the temple. So when He had looked around at all things, as the hour was already late, He went out to Bethany with the twelve. Now the next day, when they had come out from Bethany, He was hungry. And seeing from afar a fig tree having leaves, He went to see if perhaps He would find something on it. When He came to it, He found nothing but leaves, for it was not the season for figs. In response Jesus said to it, "Let no one eat fruit from you ever again." And His disciples heard it.*
> (Mark 11:11–14)

The fig tree had dried up from the roots (v. 20). We may think we have faith in God, but we must not doubt in our hearts. *"Whatever things you ask when you pray, believe that you receive them, and you will have them"* (v. 24). This is a very wonderful verse.

A Living Faith

Victory through the Word

The great theme of this discussion is the theme of faith, so I will talk about faith. Your inactivity must be brought to a place of victory. Inactivity—what wavers, what hesitates, what fears instead of having faith—closes up everything, because it doubts instead of believing God. What is faith? Faith is the living principle of the Word of God. It is life; it produces life; it changes life. Oh, that God today might give us a real knowledge of the Book! What is in it? There is life in it. God wants us to feed on the Book, the living Word, the precious Word of God.

All the wonderful things that Jesus did were done so that people might be changed and made like Him. Oh, to be like Him in thought, act, and plan! He went about His Father's business and was eaten up with the zeal of His house (Ps. 69:9). I am beginning to understand 1 John 3:2: *"Beloved, now we are children of God; and it has not yet been revealed what we shall be, but we know that when He is revealed, we shall be like Him, for we shall see Him as He is."* As I feed on the Word of God, my whole body will be changed by the process of the power of the Son of God.

> *But if the Spirit of Him who raised Jesus from the dead dwells in you, He who raised Christ from the dead will also give life to your mortal bodies through His Spirit who dwells in you.*
> (Rom. 8:11)

The Lord dwells in a humble and contrite heart and makes His way into the dry places, so if you

129

open up to Him, He will flood you with His life. But be sure to remember that a little bit of sin will spoil a whole life. You can never cleanse sin; you can never purify sin; you can never be strong if in sin; you will never have a vision while in sin. Revelation stops when sin comes in. The human spirit must come to an end, but the Spirit of Christ must be alive and active. You must die to the human spirit, and then God will quicken your mortal body and make it alive. Without holiness no man will see God (Heb. 12:14).

The Divine Power of Faith

We have a wonderful subject. What is it? Faith. Faith is an inward operation of that divine power that dwells in the contrite heart and can lay hold of the things not seen. Faith is a divine act; faith is God in the soul. God operates by His Son and transforms the natural into the supernatural.

Faith is active, never dormant. Faith lays hold; faith is the hand of God; faith is the power of God. Faith never fears; faith lives amid the greatest conflict; faith is always active; faith moves even things that cannot be moved. God fills us with His divine power, and sin is dethroned. *"The just shall live by faith"* (Rom. 1:17). You cannot live by faith until you are just and righteous. You cannot live by faith if you are unholy or dishonest.

The Lord was looking for fruit on the tree. He found *"nothing but leaves"* (Mark 11:13). There are thousands of people like that. They dress up like Christians, but it is all leaves. *"By this My Father is glorified, that you bear much fruit"* (John 15:8). The

Lord has no way in which to get fruit except through us. We cannot be ordinary people. To be saved is to be an extraordinary man, an exposition of God. When Jesus was talking about the new life, He said, *"Unless one is born again* [of God], *he cannot see the kingdom of God....That which is born of the flesh is flesh, and that which is born of the Spirit is spirit"* (John 3:3, 6).

In order to understand His fullness, we must be filled with the Holy Spirit. God has a measure for us that cannot be measured. I am invited into this measure: the measure of the Lord Jesus Christ in me. When you are in this relationship, sin is dethroned, but you cannot purify yourself. It is by the blood of Jesus Christ, God's Son, that you are cleansed from all sin.

When Jesus saw nothing but leaves, He said to this tree: *"'Let no one eat fruit from you ever again.' And His disciples heard it"* (Mark 11:14). The next morning as they passed the same place, they saw the fig tree dried up from the roots (v. 20). You never see a tree dry up from the roots. Even a little plant will dry from the top. But God's Son had spoken to the tree, and it could not live. He said to them, *"Have faith in God"* (v. 22).

We are His life; we are members of His body. The Spirit is in us, and there is no way to abide in the secret place of the Lord except by holiness.

Be filled with the Word of God. *"For the word of God is living and powerful, and sharper than any two-edged sword, piercing even to the division of soul and spirit, and of joints and marrow"* (Heb. 4:12). Listen, those of you who have stiff knees and stiff arms today, you can get a tonic by the Word of God that will loosen your joints and that will divide even your joints and marrow. You cannot move your knee if there is no marrow there, but the Word of God can bring marrow into your bones.

Is there anything else? One of the greatest things in the Word of God is that it discerns the thoughts and intentions of the heart. Oh, that you may all allow the Word of God to have perfect victory in your bodies so that they may be tingling through and through with God's divine power! Divine life does not belong to this world but to the kingdom of heaven, and the kingdom of heaven is within you.

God wants to purify our minds until we can bear all things, believe all things, hope all things, and endure all things (1 Cor. 13:7). God dwells in you, but you cannot have this divine power until you live and walk in the Holy Spirit, until the power of the new life is greater than the old life.

Jesus said to His disciples, "If you will believe in your hearts, not only will the tree wither, but the mountain will also be removed." (See Matthew 21:21.) God wants us to move mountains. Anything that appears to be like a mountain can be moved: the mountains of difficulty, the mountains of perplexity, the mountains of depression or depravity— things that have bound you for years. Sometimes things appear as though they could not be moved, but you can believe in your heart and stand on the Word of God, and God's Word will never be defeated.

Notice again this Scripture: *"Whatever things you ask when you pray, believe that you receive them, and you will have them"* (Mark 11:24). First, believe that you get them, and then you will have them. That is the difficulty with people. They say, "Well, if I could feel I had it, I would know I had it." But you must believe it, and then the feeling will come. You must believe it because of the Word of God. God wants to work in you a real heart faith. I want you to know that God has a real remedy for all your ailments. There is power to set everybody free.

13

The Blessed Reality of God

*Now faith is the substance of things hoped for, the
evidence of things not seen. For by it the elders
obtained a good testimony.*
—Hebrews 11:1–2

od has moved me to discuss the marvelous,
glorious reality of God's Word. How great our
faith should be, for we cannot be saved except
by faith. We cannot be kept except by faith. We can
only be baptized by faith, and we will be caught up
by faith; therefore, what a blessed reality is faith in
the living God.

The Nature and the Word of God

What is faith? It is the very nature of God. Faith
is the Word of God. It is the personal inward flow of
divine favor, which moves in every fiber of our being
until our whole nature is so quickened that we live
by faith, we move by faith, and we are going to be
caught up to glory by faith, for faith is the victory!
Faith is the glorious knowledge of a personal presence

within you, changing you from strength to strength, from glory to glory, until you get to the place where you walk with God, and God thinks and speaks through you by the power of the Holy Spirit. Oh, it is grand; it is glorious!

God wants us to have far more than what we can handle and see, and so He speaks of *"the substance of things hoped for, the evidence of things not seen."* With the eye of faith, we may see the blessing in all its beauty and grandeur. God's Word is from everlasting to everlasting (Ps. 90:2), and *"faith is the substance."*

If I would give some woman a piece of cloth, scissors, needle, and thread, she could produce a garment. Why? Because she had the material. If I would provide some man with wood, a saw, a hammer, and nails, he could produce a box. Why? Because he had the material. But God, without material, spoke the Word and produced this world with all its beauty. There was no material there, but the Word of God called it into being by His creative force. With the knowledge that you are born again by this incorruptible Word, which lives and abides forever (1 Pet. 1:23), you know that within you is this living, definite hope, greater than yourself, more powerful than any dynamic force in the world, for faith works in you by the power of the new creation of God in Christ Jesus.

Therefore, with the audacity of faith, we should throw ourselves into the omnipotence of God's divine plan, for God has said to us, *"If you can believe, all things are possible to him who believes"* (Mark 9:23). It is possible for the power of God to be so manifest in your human life that you will never be as you were before, for you will be always going forward from victory to victory, for faith knows no defeat.

The Word of God will bring you into a wonderful place of rest in faith. God intends for you to have a clear conception of what faith is, how faith came, and how it remains. Faith is in the divine plan, for it brings you to the open door so that you might enter in. You must have an open door, for you cannot open the door. It is God who does it, but He wants you to be ready to step in and claim His promises of all the divine manifestations of power in the name of Christ Jesus. It is only thus that you will be able to meet and conquer the enemy, for *"He who is in you is greater than he who is in the world"* (1 John 4:4).

Living faith brings glorious power and personality; it gives divine ability, for it is by faith that Christ is manifested in your mortal flesh by the Word of God. I do not want you to miss the knowledge that you have heard from God, and I want you to realize that God has so changed you that all weakness, fear, inability—everything that has made you a failure—has passed away. Faith has power to make you what God wants you to be; only you must be ready to step into the plan and believe His Word.

A Triumphant Position in God

The first manifestation of God's plan was the cross of Calvary. You may refuse it; You may resist it; but God, who loves you with an everlasting love, has followed you through life and will follow you with His great grace, so that He may bring you to a knowledge of this great salvation.

God, in His own plan for your eternal good, may have brought something into your life that is distasteful, something that is causing you to feel desperate or to feel that your life is worthless. What does it mean? It means that the Spirit of God is showing you your own weakness so that you might cry out to Him, and when you do, He will show you the cross of redemption. Then God will give you faith to believe, for faith is the gift of God.

God, who has given us this faith, has a wonderful plan for our lives. Do you remember when God brought you to this place of salvation, how the faith He gave you brought a great desire to do something for Him, and then He showed you that wonderful open door? I was saved over sixty-seven years ago, and I have never lost the witness of the Spirit. If you will not allow your human nature to crush your faith and interfere with God's plan in its wonderful divine setting, you will mount up like the eagles (Isa. 40:31). Oh, the wonderful effectiveness of God's perfect plan working in us with the divine Trinity flowing through humanity, changing our very nature to the extent that we cannot disbelieve but must act faith, talk faith, and in faith sing praises unto the Lord! There is no room for anything that is not faith, for we have passed beyond the natural plane into a new atmosphere: God enclosed and enclosing us.

Faith is an increasing position, always triumphant. It is not a place of poverty but of wealth. If you always live in fruitfulness, you will always have plenty. What does it say in our text? *"The elders obtained a good testimony"*! The man who lives in faith always has a good testimony. The Acts of the Apostles were written because the lives of the apostles bore the fruit of active faith. To them, faith was an everyday fact. If your life is in the divine order, you will not only have living, active faith, but you will also always be building up someone else in faith.

What is the good of preaching without faith? God intends that we should so live in this glorious sphere of the power of God that we will always be in a position to tell people of the act that brought the fact. You must act before you can see the fact. What is the good of praying for the sick without faith? You must believe that God will not deny Himself, for the Word of God cannot be denied. I believe this message is given in divine order so that you may no longer be in a place of doubt but will realize that *"faith is the substance"*! Beloved, even with all the faith we have, we are not even so much as touching the hem of God's plan for us. It is like going to the seashore and dipping your toe in the water, with the great vast ocean before you. God wants us to rise on the crest of the tide and not keep paddling along the shore. Oh, to be connected with that sublime power, that human nature may know God and the glory of the manifestation of Christ!

The Word of God is eternal and cannot be broken. You cannot improve on the Word of God, for it is life, and it produces life. Listen! God has begotten you to a living hope (1 Pet. 1:3). You are born again of the Word that created worlds. If you dare to believe, such belief is powerful. God wants us to be powerful, a people of faith, a purified people, a people who will launch out in God and dare to trust Him in glorious faith, which always takes you beyond what is commonplace to an abiding place in God.

14

The Substance of Things Hoped For

ebrews chapter eleven is a wonderful passage; in fact, all the Word of God is wonderful. It is not only wonderful, but it also has power to change conditions. Any natural condition can be changed by the Word of God, which is a supernatural power. In the Word of God is the breath, the nature, and the power of the living God, and His power works in every person who dares to believe His Word. There is life though the power of it, and as we receive the Word of faith, we receive the nature of God Himself.

It is as we lay hold of God's promises in simple faith that we become partakers of the divine nature. As we receive the Word of God, we come right into touch with a living force, a power that changes nature into grace, a power that makes dead things live, and a power that is of God, that will be manifested in our flesh. This power has come forth with its glory to transform us by divine acts into sons of God, to make us like the Son of God, by the Spirit of God who moves us on from grace to grace and from glory to glory as our faith rests in this living Word.

Faith Is a Foundation

It is important that we have a foundation truth, something greater than ourselves, on which to rest. In Hebrews 12:2 we read, *"Looking unto Jesus, the author and finisher of our faith."* Jesus is our life, and He is the power of our life. We see in the fifth chapter of Acts that as soon as Peter was let out of prison, the Word of God came: *"Go...speak...all the words of this life"* (v. 20).

There is only one Book that has life. In this Word we find Him who came that we might have life and have it more abundantly (John 10:10), and by faith this life is imparted to us. When we come into this life by divine faith—and we must realize that it is by grace we are saved through faith, and that it is not of ourselves but is the gift of God (Eph. 2:8)—we become partakers of this life. This Word is greater than anything else. There is no darkness in it at all. Anyone who dwells in this Word is able under all circumstances to say that he is willing to come to the light so that his deeds may be seen (John 3:21). But outside of the Word is darkness, and the manifestations of darkness will never desire to come to the light because their deeds are evil. But the moment we are saved by the power of the Word of God, we love the light and the truth. The inexpressible divine power, force, passion, and fire that we receive are of God. Drink, my beloved, drink deeply of this Source of life.

"Faith is the substance of things hoped for" (Heb. 11:1). Someone said to me one day, "I would

not believe in anything I could not handle and see." Everything you can handle and see is temporary and will perish with the using. But the things not seen are eternal and will not fade away. Are you dealing with tangible things or with the things that are eternal, that are facts, that are made real to faith? Thank God that through the knowledge of the truth of the Son of God I have within me a greater power, a mightier working, an inward impact of life, of power, of vision, and of truth more real than anyone can know who lives in the realm of the tangible. God manifests Himself to the person who dares to believe.

But there is something more beautiful than that. As we receive divine life in the new birth, we receive a nature that delights to do the will of God. As we believe the Word of God, a well of water springs up within our hearts. A spring is always better than a pump. But I know that a spring is apt to be outclassed when we get to the baptism of the Holy Spirit. It was a spring to the woman at the well, but with the person who has the Holy Spirit, it is flowing rivers. Do you have these flowing rivers? To be filled with the Holy Spirit is to be filled with the Executive of the Godhead, who brings to us all that the Father has and all that the Son desires, and we should be so in the Spirit that God can cause us to move with His authority and reign by His divine ability.

I thank God that He baptizes with the Holy Spirit. I know He did it for me because others heard me speak in tongues, and then I heard myself. That was a scriptural work, and I don't want anything else, because I must be the epistle of God. A whole epistle of the life, of the power, and of the resurrection of my

Lord Jesus must be emanating through my body. There are wonderful things happening through this divine union with God Himself.

"[God] *has in these last days spoken to us by His Son, whom He has appointed heir of all things, through whom also He made the worlds"* (Heb. 1:2). By this divine Person, this Word, this Son, God made all things. Notice that it says that He made the worlds by this Person and made them out of the things that were not there. Everything we see was made by this divine Son. I want you to see that as you receive the Son of God, and as Christ dwells in your heart by faith, there is a divine force, the power of limitless possibilities, within you. As a result of this incoming Christ, God wants to do great things through you. By faith, if we receive and accept His Son, God brings us into sonship, and not only into sonship but into joint-heirship, into sharing together with Him all that the Son possesses.

We Have Divine Authority

I am more and more convinced every day I live that very few who are saved by the grace of God have a right conception of how great their authority is over darkness, demons, death, and every power of the enemy. It is a real joy when we realize our inheritance along this line.

I was speaking like this one day, and someone said, "I have never heard anything like this before. How many months did it take you to think up that sermon?"

I said, "My brother, God pressed my wife from time to time to get me to preach, and I promised her

I would preach. I used to labor hard for a week to think something up, then give out the text and sit down and say, 'I am done.' Oh, brother, I have given up thinking things up. They all come down. And the sermons that come down stop down, then go back, because the Word of God says His Word will not return to Him void (Isa. 55:11). But if you get anything up, it will not stay up very long, and when it goes down, it takes you down with it."

The sons of God are made manifest in this present earth to destroy the power of the devil. To be saved by the power of God is to be brought from the realm of the ordinary into the extraordinary, from the natural into the divine.

Do you remember the day when the Lord laid His hands on you? You say, "I could not do anything except praise the Lord." Well, that was only the beginning. Where are you today? The divine plan is that you increase until you receive the measureless fullness of God. You do not have to say, "I tell you it was wonderful when I was baptized with the Holy Spirit." If you have to look back to the past to make me know you are baptized, then you are backslidden.

If the beginning was good, it ought to be better day by day, until everybody is fully convinced that you are filled with the might of God in the Spirit, *"filled with all the fullness of God"* (Eph. 3:19). *"Do not be drunk with wine, in which is dissipation; but be filled with the Spirit"* (Eph. 5:18). I don't want anything other than being full and fuller and fuller, until I am overflowing like a great big vat. Do you realize that if you have been created anew and born again by the Word of God that there is within you the word of power and the same light and life as the Son of God Himself had?

God wants to flow through you with measureless power of divine utterance and grace until your whole body is a flame of fire. God intends each soul in Pentecost to be a live wire—not a monument, but a movement. So many people have been baptized with the Holy Spirit; there was a movement, but they have become monuments, and you cannot move them. God, wake us out of sleep lest we should become indifferent to the glorious truth and the breath of the almighty power of God. We must be the light and salt of the earth (Matt. 5:13–14), with the whole armor of God upon us (Eph. 6:11). It would be a serious thing if the enemies were about and we had to go back and get our shoes. It would be a serious thing if we had on no breastplate.

How can we be furnished with the armor? Take it by faith. Jump in, stop in, and never come out, for this is a baptism to be lost in, where you only know one thing and that is the desire of God at all times. The baptism in the Spirit should be an ever increasing endowment of power, an ever increasing enlargement of grace. Oh, Father, grant to us a real look into the glorious liberty You have designed for the children of God, who are delivered from this present world, separated, sanctified, and made suitable for Your use, whom You have designed to be filled with all Your fullness.

Just Believe!

Nothing has hurt me so much as this, to see so-called believers have so much unbelief in them that it is hard to move them. There is no difficulty in praying for a sinner to be healed, but when you touch the "believer," he comes back and says, "You did not pray for my legs." I say you are healed all over if you believe. Everything is possible to those who believe (Mark 9:23). God will not fail His Word, whatever you are. Suppose that all the people in the world did not believe; that would make no difference to God's Word; it would be the same. You cannot alter God's Word. It is from everlasting to everlasting, and they who believe in it will be like Mount Zion, which cannot be moved.

I was preaching on faith one time, and there was a man in the audience who said three times, "I won't believe." I kept right on preaching because that made no difference to me. I am prepared for a fight any day, the fight of faith. We must keep the faith that has been committed to us. I went on preaching, and the man shouted out, "I won't believe." As he left, he cried out again, "I won't believe."

The next day a message came saying there was a man in the meeting the night before who said out loud three times, "I won't believe," and as soon as he got outside, the Spirit said to him, "You will be mute because you did not believe." It was the same Spirit that came to Zacharias and said, *"You will be mute and not able to speak until the day these things take place, because you did not believe my words"* (Luke 1:20).

I believe in a hell. Who is in hell? The unbeliever. If you want to go to hell, all you need to do is to disbelieve the Word of God. The unbelievers are there. Thank God they are there, for they are no good for any society. I said to the leader of that meeting, "You go and see this man and find out if these things are so."

He went to the house, and the first one to greet him was the man's wife. He said, "Is it true that your husband declared three times in the meeting that he would not believe and now he cannot speak?"

She burst into tears and said, "Go and see." He went into the room and saw the man's mouth in a terrible state. The man got a piece of paper and wrote, "I had an opportunity to believe. I refused to believe, and now I cannot believe and cannot speak." The greatest sin in the world is to disbelieve God's Word. We are not of those who draw back, but we are of those who believe (Heb. 10:39); for God's Word is a living Word, and it always acts.

One day a stylishly dressed lady came to our meeting and on up to the platform. Under her arm, going down underneath her dress, was a concealed crutch that nobody could see. She had been helpless in one leg for twenty years, had heard of what God was doing, and wanted to be prayed for. As soon as we prayed for her, she exclaimed, "What have you done with my leg?" Three times she said it, and then we saw that the crutch was loose and hanging and that she was standing straight up.

The lady that was interpreting for me said to her, "We have done nothing with your leg. If anything has been done, it is God who has done it."

She answered, "I have been lame and used a crutch for twenty years, but my leg is perfect now." We did not suggest that she get down at the altar and thank God; she fell down among the others and cried for mercy. I find that when God touches us, it is a divine touch, life, and power, and it thrills and quickens the body so that people know it is God. Then conviction comes, and they cry for mercy. Praise God for anything that brings people to the throne of grace.

God heals by the power of His Word. But the most important thing is, Are you saved? Do you know the Lord? Are you prepared to meet God? You may be an invalid as long as you live, but you may be saved by the power of God. You may have a strong, healthy body but may go straight to hell because you know nothing of the grace of God and salvation. Thank God I was saved in a moment, the moment I believed, and God will do the same for you.

God means by this divine power within you to make you follow after the mind of the Spirit by the Word of God until you are entirely changed by the power of it. You might come on this platform and say, "Wigglesworth, is there anything you can look up to God and ask Him for in your body?" I will say now that I have a body in perfect condition and have nothing to ask for, and I am sixty-five. It was not always so. This body was a frail, helpless body, but God fulfilled His Word to me according to Isaiah and Matthew: He took my infirmities and my diseases, my sicknesses, and by His stripes I am healed (Matt. 8:17; Isa. 53:5).

It is wonderful to go here and there and not even notice that you have a body because it is not a hindrance to you. He took our infirmities. He bore our sickness; He came to heal our brokenheartedness. Jesus wants us to come forth in divine likeness, in resurrection force, in the power of the Spirit, to walk in faith and understand His Word. That is what He meant when He said He would give us power over all the power of the enemy. He will subdue all things until everything comes into perfect harmony with His will. Is He reigning over your affections, desires, and will? If so, when He reigns, you will be subject to His reigning power. He will be the authority over the whole situation. When He reigns, everything must be subservient to His divine plan and will for us.

See what the Word of God says: *"No one can say that Jesus is Lord except by the Holy Spirit"* (1 Cor. 12:3). *"Lord!"* Bless God forever. Oh, for Him to be Lord and Master! For Him to rule and control! For Him to be filling your whole body with the plan of truth! Because you are in Christ Jesus, all things are subject to Him. It is lovely, and God wants to make it so to you. When you get there, you will find divine power continually working. I absolutely believe that no man comes into the place of revelation and activity of the gifts of the Spirit except by this fulfilled promise of Jesus that He will baptize us in the Holy Spirit.

God Knows and Can Heal

I was taken to see a beautiful nine-year-old boy who was lying on a bed. The mother and father were distraught because he had been lying there for months. They had to lift and feed him; he was like a statue with flashing eyes. As soon as I entered the place, the Lord revealed to me the cause of the trouble, so I said to the mother, "The Lord shows me there is something wrong with his stomach."

She said, "Oh no, we have had two physicians, and they say it is paralysis of the mind."

I said, "God reveals to me it is his stomach."

"Oh, no, it isn't. These physicians ought to know, they have X rayed him."

The gentleman who brought me there said to the mother, "You have sent for this man; you have been the means of his coming; now don't you stand out against him. This man knows what he has got to do."

But Dr. Jesus knows more than that. He knows everything. You have no need to ring the bell for doctors. All you have to do is ring your bell for Jesus, and He will come down. Divine things are so much better than human things and just at your call. Who will interfere with the divine mind of the Spirit that has all revelation, that understands the whole condition of life? The Word of God declares He knows all things (1 John 3:20) and is well acquainted with the manifestation of our bodies, for everything is naked and open before Him to whom we must give account (Heb. 4:13). Having the mind of the Spirit, we understand what the will of God is. I prayed over this boy and laid my hands on his stomach. He became sick and vomited a worm thirteen inches long and was perfectly restored. Who knows? God knows. When will we come into the knowledge of God? When we cease from our own mind and allow ourselves to become clothed with the mind and authority of the mighty God.

Unbelief Hinders God's Power

The Spirit of God wants us to understand there is nothing that can interfere with our coming into perfect blessing except unbelief. Unbelief is a terrible hindrance. As soon as we are willing to allow the Holy Spirit to have His way, we will find that great things will happen all the time. But oh, how much of our own human reason we have to get rid of, how much human planning we have to become divorced from. What would happen right now if everybody believed God? I love the thought that God the Holy Spirit wants to emphasize the truth that if we will only yield ourselves to the divine plan, He is right there to bring forth the mystery of truth.

How many of us believe the Word? It is easy to quote it, but it is more important to have it than to quote it. It is very easy for me to quote, *"Now we are children of God"* (1 John 3:2), but it is more important for me to know whether I am a son of God. When the Son was on the earth, He was recognized by the people who heard Him. *"No man ever spoke like [Him]"* (John 7:46). His word was with power, and that word came to pass. Sometimes you have quoted, *"He who is in you is greater than he who is in the world"* (1 John 4:4), and you could tell just where to find it. But brother, is it so? Can demons remain in your presence? You have to be greater than demons. Can disease lodge in the body that you touch? You have to be greater than the disease. Can anything in the world stand against you and hold its place if it is a fact that He who is in you is greater than he who is in the world? Do we dare stand on the Word of God and face the facts of the difficulties before us?

"Faith is the substance of things hoped for" (Heb. 11:1). Faith is the Word. You were begotten of the Word; the Word is in you; the life of the Son is in you; and God wants you to believe.

15

The Way of Faith

n Romans 4:16 we read, *"It is of faith that it might be according to grace,"* meaning that we can open the door, and God will come in. What will happen if we really open the door by faith? God is greater than our thoughts. He puts it to us, *"exceedingly abundantly above all that we ask or think"* (Eph. 3:20). When we ask a lot, God says "more." Are we ready for the "more"? And then the "much more"? We must be, or we will miss it.

We may be so clothed with the Spirit of the Lord in the morning that it will be a tonic for the whole day. God can so thrill us with new life that nothing ordinary or small will satisfy us after that. There is a great place for us in God where we won't be satisfied with small things. We won't have any satisfaction unless the fire falls, and whenever we pray we will have the assurance that what we are about to pray for is going to follow the moment we open our mouths. Oh, this praying in the Spirit! This great plan of God for us! In a moment we can go right in. In where? Into His will. Then all things will be well.

You can't get anything while we are asleep these days. The world is always awake, and we should always be awake to what God has for us. Awake to take! Awake to hold it after we get it! How much can you take? We know that God is more willing to give than we are to receive. How will we dare to be asleep when the Spirit commands us to take everything on the table? It is the greatest banquet that ever was and ever will be—the table where all you take only leaves more behind. It is a fullness that cannot be exhausted! How many are prepared for abundance?

The Word Must Come to Pass

And Jesus went into Jerusalem and into the temple. So when He had looked around at all things, as the hour was already late, He went out to Bethany with the twelve. Now the next day, when they had come out from Bethany, He was hungry. And seeing from afar a fig tree having leaves, He went to see if perhaps He would find something on it. When He came to it, He found nothing but leaves, for it was not the season for figs. In response Jesus said to it, "Let no one eat fruit from you ever again." And His disciples heard it.

(Mark 11:11–14)

Jesus was sent from God to meet the world's needs. Jesus lived to minister life by the words He spoke. He said to Philip, *"He who has seen Me has seen the Father....The words that I speak to you I do not speak on my own authority; but the Father who dwells in Me"* (John 14:9–10). I am persuaded that if we are filled with His words of life and the Holy Spirit, and Christ is made manifest in our mortal flesh, then the Holy Spirit can really move us with His life and His words until as He was, so are we in the world. We are receiving our life from God, and it is always kept in tremendous activity, working in our whole natures as we live in perfect contact with God.

Jesus spoke, and everything He said must come to pass. That is the great plan. When we are filled only with the Holy Spirit, and we won't allow the Word of God to be taken away by what we hear or by what we read, then comes the inspiration, then the life, then the activity, then the glory! Oh, to live in it! To live in it is to be moved by it. To live in it is to be moved so that we will have God's life and God's personality in the human body.

By the grace of God I want to impart the Word and bring you into a place where you will dare to act upon the plan of the Word, to so breathe life by the power of the Word that it is impossible for you to go on under any circumstances without His provision. The most difficult things that come to us are to our advantage from God's side. When we come to the place of impossibilities, it is the grandest place for us to see the possibilities of God. Put this right in your mind, and never forget it. You will never be of any importance to God until you venture in the impossible. God wants people to be daring, and I do not mean foolishly daring. *"Be filled with the Spirit"* (Eph. 5:18). When we are filled with the Spirit, we are not so much concerned about the secondary thing. We are concerned about the first thing, which is God's.

Everything evil, everything unclean, everything satanic in any way, is an objectionable thing to God, and we are to live above it, destroy it, and not allow it to have any place. Jesus didn't let the devil answer back. We must reach the place where we will not allow anything to interfere with the plan of God.

Jesus and His disciples came to the tree. It looked beautiful. It had the appearance of fruit, but when He came to it, He found nothing but leaves. He was very disappointed. Looking at the tree, He spoke to it. His destructive power is shown forth here: *"Let no one eat fruit from you ever again"* (Mark 11:14). The next day they were passing by the same way, and the disciples saw the tree *"dried up from the roots"* (v. 20). They said to Jesus, *"Look! The fig tree which You cursed has withered away"* (v. 21). And Jesus said, *"Have faith in God"* (v. 22).

As I said previously, there isn't a person who has ever seen a tree dried from the roots. Trees always show the first signs of death right at the top. But the Master had spoken. The Master dealt with a natural thing to reveal to these disciples a supernatural plan. If He spoke, it would have to obey. And God, the Holy Spirit, wants us to understand clearly that we are the mouthpieces of God and are here for His divine plan. We may allow the natural mind to dethrone that, but in the measure we do, we won't come into the treasure that God has for us.

The Word of God must have first place. It must not have a second place. In any measure that we doubt the Word of God, from that moment we have ceased to thrive spiritually and actively. The Word of God is not only to be looked at and read, but also received as the Word of God to become life right within our life. *"Your word I have hidden in my heart, that I might not sin against You"* (Ps. 119:11).

"I give you the authority...over all the power of the enemy" (Luke 10:19). There it is. We can accept or reject it. I accept and believe it. It is a word beyond all human calculation. *"Have faith in God"* (Mark 11:22). These disciples were in the Master's school. They were the men who were to turn the world upside down. As we receive the Word, we will never be the same; if we dare to act as the Word goes forth and are not afraid, then God will honor us.

"The LORD of hosts is with us; the God of Jacob is our refuge" (Ps. 46:7). Jacob was the weakest of all, in any way you like to take it. But God is the God of Jacob, and He is our God. So we may likewise have our names changed to Israel.

As the Lord Jesus injected this wonderful word, *"Have faith in God"* (Mark 11:22), into the disciples, He began to show how it was to be. Looking around Him, He saw the mountains, and He began to give a practical application. A truth means nothing unless it moves us. We can have our minds filled a thousand times, but it must get into our hearts if there are to be any results. All inspiration is in the heart. All compassion is in the heart.

Looking at the mountains, Jesus said,

> *Whoever says to this mountain, "Be removed and be cast into the sea," and does not doubt in his heart, but believes that those things he*

says will be done, he will have whatever he says. (Mark 11: 23)

That is the barometer. You know exactly where you are. The man knows when he prays. If his heart is right, how it leaps! Any man who does not hate sin is no good for God and never makes progress in God. You are never safe. But there is a place in God where you can love righteousness and where you can hate iniquity until the Word of God is a light in your being, quickening every fiber of your body, thrilling your whole nature. The pure in heart see God (Matt. 5:8). Believe in the heart! What a word! If I believe in my heart, God says I can begin to speak, and whatever I say will come to pass (Mark 11:23).

There Is No Defeat with God

Here is an act of believing in the heart. I was called to Halifax, England, to pray for a lady missionary. I found that it was an urgent call. I could see there was an absence of faith, and I could see there was death.

I said to the woman, "How are you?"

She said, "I have faith," in a very weak tone of voice.

"Faith? Why are you dying? Brother Walshaw, is she dying?"

"Yes."

To a friend standing by, "Is she dying?"

"Yes."

Now I believe there is something in a heart that is against defeat, and this is the faith that God has given to us. I said to her, "In the name of Jesus, now believe, and you'll live." She said, "I believe," and God sent life from her head to her feet. They dressed her, and she lived.

"Have faith" (Mark 11:22). It isn't saying you have faith. It is he who believes in his heart. It is a grasping of the eternal God. Faith is God in the human vessel. *"This is the victory that has overcome the world; our faith"* (1 John 5:4). He who believes overcomes the world. *"Faith comes by hearing, and hearing by the word of God"* (Rom. 10:17). He who believes in his heart—can you imagine anything easier than that? He who believes in his heart! What is the process? Death! No one who believes in his heart can live according to the world. He dies to everything worldly. He who loves the world is not of God. You can measure the whole thing up and examine yourself to see if you have faith. Faith is a life. Faith enables you to lay hold of what is and get it out of the way for God to bring in something that is not.

Just before I left home I was in Norway. A woman wrote to me from England saying she had been operated on for cancer three years before but that it was now coming back. She was living in constant dread of the whole thing, since the operation was so painful. She asked if it would it possible to see me when I returned to England. I wrote that I would be passing through London on the twentieth of June. If she would like to meet me at the hotel, I would pray for her. She replied that she would go to London to be there to meet me.

When I met this woman, I saw she was in great pain, and I have great sympathy for people who have tried to get relief and have failed. If you preachers lose your compassion, you can stop preaching, for it won't be any good. You will only be successful as a preacher if you let your heart become filled with the compassion of Jesus. As soon as I saw her, I entered into the state of her mind. I saw how distressed she was. She came to me in a mournful spirit, and her whole face was downcast. I said to her, "There are two things that are going to happen today. One is that you are to know that you are saved."

"Oh, if I could only know I was saved," she said.

"There is another thing. You have to go out of this hotel without a pain, without a trace of the cancer."

Then I began with the Word—oh, this wonderful Word! We do not have to go up to bring Him down; nor do we have to go down to bring Him up (Rom. 10:6–7). *"'The word is near you, in your mouth and in your heart' (that is, the word of faith which we preach)"* (v. 8). I said, "Believe that He took your sins when He died at the cross. Believe that when He was buried, it was for you. Believe that when He arose, it was for you. And now He is sitting at God's right hand for you. If you can believe in your heart and confess with your mouth, you will be saved."

She looked at me saying, "Oh, it is going all through my body. I know I am saved now. If He comes today, I'll go. How I have dreaded the thought of His coming all my life! But if He comes today, I know I will be ready."

The first thing was finished. Now for the second. I laid my hands upon her in the name of Jesus, believing in my heart that I could say what I wanted and it would be done. I said, "In the name of Jesus, I cast this out."

She jumped up. "Two things have happened," she said. "I am saved, and now the cancer is gone."

> Faith will stand amid the wrecks of time,
> Faith unto eternal glories climb;
> Only count the promise true,
> And the Lord will stand by you.
> Faith will win the victory every time!

So many people have nervous trouble. I'll tell you how to get rid of your nervous trouble. I have something in my bag, one dose of which will cure you: *"I am the LORD who heals you"* (Exod. 15:26). How this wonderful Word of God changes the situation!

"Perfect love casts out fear" (1 John 4:18). *"There is no fear in love"* (v. 18). I have tested that so often, casting out the whole condition of fear, and the whole situation has been changed. We have a big God, only He has to be absolutely and exclusively trusted. The people who really do believe God are strong, and the righteous *"will be stronger and stronger"* (Job 17:9).

At the close of a certain meeting, a man said to me, "You have helped everybody but me. I wish you would help me."

"What's the trouble with you?"

"I cannot sleep because of nervous trouble. My wife says she has not known me to have a full night's sleep for three years. I am just shattered."

Anyone could tell he was. I put my hands upon him and said, "Brother, I believe in my heart. Go home and sleep in the name of Jesus."

"I can't sleep."

"Go home and sleep in the name of Jesus."

"I can't sleep."

The lights were being put out, and I took the man by the coat collar and said, "Don't talk to me anymore." That was sufficient.

He went after that. When he got home, his mother and wife both said to him, "What has happened?"

"Nothing. He helped everybody but me."

"Surely he said something to you."

"He told me to come home and sleep in the name of Jesus, but you know I can't sleep in anything."

His wife urged him to do what I had said, and he had scarcely got his head on the pillow before the Lord put him to sleep. The next morning he was still asleep. She began to make a noise in the bedroom to awaken him, but he did not waken. Sunday morning he was still asleep. She did what every good wife would do. She decided to make a good Sunday dinner and then awaken him.

After the dinner was prepared, she went up to him and put her hand on his shoulder and shook him, saying, "It is time for you to wake up." From that night that man never had any more nervousness.

A man came to me for whom I prayed. Then I asked, "Are you sure you are perfectly healed?"

"Well," he said, "there is just a little pain in my shoulder."

"Do you know what that is?" I asked him. "That is unbelief. Were you saved before you believed or after?"

"After."

"You will be healed after."

"It is all right now," he said. It was all right before, but he hadn't believed.

The Word of God is for us. It is by faith, so that it might be by grace.

16

The Way to Overcome

ow let's take a look at 1 John 5. The greatest weakness in the world is unbelief. The greatest power is the faith that works by love. Love, mercy, and grace are bound eternally to faith. Fear is the opposite of faith, but *"there is no fear in love"* (1 John 4:18). Those whose hearts are filled with a divine faith and love have no question in their hearts as to being caught up when Jesus comes.

The world is filled with fear, torment, remorse, and brokenness, but faith and love are sure to overcome. *"Who is he who overcomes the world, but he who believes that Jesus is the Son of God?"* (1 John 5:5). God has established the earth and humanity on the lines of faith. As you come into line, fear is cast out, the Word of God comes into operation, and you find bedrock. All the promises are *"Yes"* and *"Amen"* to those who believe (2 Cor. 1:20).

When you have faith in Christ, the love of God is so real that you feel you could do anything for Jesus. Whoever believes, loves. *"We love Him because He first loved us"* (1 John 4:19). When did He love us? When we were in the mire. What did He say? *"Your sins are forgiven you"* (Luke 5:20). Why did He say it? Because He loved us. What for? That He might bring many sons into glory (Heb. 2:10). What was His purpose? That we might be with Him forever.

The whole pathway is an education for this high vocation and calling. How glorious this hidden mystery of love is! For our sins there is the double blessing. *"Whatever is born of God overcomes the world. And this is the victory...our faith"* (1 John 5:4). To believe is to overcome.

I am heir to all the promises because I believe. It is a great heritage. I overcome because I believe the truth, and the truth makes me free (John 8:32). Christ is the root and source of our faith, and because He is in our faith, what we believe for will come to pass. There is no wavering. This is the principle: he who believes is definite. A definite faith brings a definite experience and a definite utterance.

There is no limit to the power God will cause to come upon those who cry to Him in faith, for God is rich to all who will call upon Him. Stake your claim for your children, your families, your coworkers, that many sons may be brought to glory. As your prayer rests upon the simple principle of faith, nothing will be impossible for you.

The root principle of all this divine overcoming faith in the human heart is Christ, and when you are grafted deeply into Him, you may win millions of lives to the faith. Jesus is the Way, the Truth, and the Life (John 14:6), the secret to every hard problem in your heart.

"Love has been perfected among us in this: that we may have boldness in the day of judgment; because as He is, so are we in this world" (1 John 4:17).

The Way to Overcome

"Everyone who has this hope in Him purifies himself" (1 John 3:3). God confirms this faith in us so that we may be refined in the world, *"not having spot or wrinkle or any such thing"* (Eph. 5:27).

It is the Lord who purifies and brings us to the place where the fire burns up the dross, and there He anoints us with fresh oil, so that at all times we may be ready for His appearing. God is separating us for Himself, just as He separated Enoch for a walk with Himself. Because of a divinely implanted faith, he had the testimony before his translation that he pleased God (Heb. 11:5). As the Day of the Lord hastens on, we, too, need to walk by faith until we overcome all things. By our simple belief in Jesus Christ, we walk right into glory.

17

Only Believe

I want you to be full of joy, enough joy to fill a deep well. If you have to make it happen, there is something wrong. If God makes it happen, there is always something right. We must be careful to see that God means something greater for us than we have ever touched.

Go Forward

I have thought a great deal about momentum. I find there is such a thing as trusting in the past. When a train has gotten to a certain place, some people get out, but some go on to the end of the journey. Let us go far enough. There is only one thing to do: stay fully aware and always be pressing on. It will not do to trust in the past. Let us go forward. When it comes to the power of momentum, the past will not do. We must have an inflow of the life of God manifested, because we are in that place of manifestation.

I want you to sing now what I sing in all my meetings: "Only Believe."

Only believe, only believe,
    All things are possible, only believe.
Only believe, only believe,
    All things are possible, only believe.

The importance of that chorus is that right there in the middle of it is that word *only*. If I can get you to see that when you can get rid of yourself and your human help and everything else and have only God behind you, then you have reached a place of great reinforcement. You have reached a place of continual success. If you help yourself—in the measure you help yourself—you will find that the life of God and the power of God are diminished.

I find so many people trying to help themselves. What God wants is for us to cling to Him absolutely and entirely. There is only one grand plan that God has for us: *"Only believe"* (Mark 5:36). If we believe, we will have absolute rest and perfect submission. When God has entirely taken charge of the situation, you are absolutely brought into everything that God has, because you dare to *"only believe"* what He says.

Conditions on God's side are always beyond your asking or thinking. The conditions on your side cannot reach the other side unless you come into a place where you can rest on the omnipotent plan of God; then His plan cannot fail to be successful. God wants me to press into your heart a living truth: only believe and have absolute rest and perfect tranquillity and allow God to absolutely take charge of the whole situation. You can then say, "God has said it, and it cannot fail." All His promises are *"Yes"* and *"Amen"* to those who believe (2 Cor. 1:20). Are you ready to sing it now? Only believe. Only believe. All things are possible; only believe.

There Is No Condemnation

Look at Romans 8:1–17. We have a tremendously big subject before us, but it will be one that will be helpful. It is in the realm of spiritual vitality. I want to speak to you on life because I find that there is nothing that is going to help you reach, press in to, or live this higher life, except this divine life, which will always help us if we yield ourselves absolutely to it. We not only get exercised by this divine light, but we are kept in perfect rest, because God is giving us rest. And it is needed in this day, for this is a day when people everywhere are becoming self-contented in natural things, and when everywhere there is no definite cry or prayer within the soul that is making people cease from everything and cry out for God and the coming of the Son.

So I am intensely eager and full of desire that I may by some means quicken or move you on to a place where you will see what the Spirit has for you. Life in Christ is absolutely different from death. Life is what people long for because of everything it has in it. Death is what people draw back from because of what it has in it. This light of the life of the Spirit, which God wants me to bring before you, is where God has designed for us to live, in freedom from the law of sin and death.

So you can see I have a great subject, which is from the divine mind of the Master. You remember what the Master said. He said that He who lives for himself will die. He who seeks to live will die, but he

171

who is willing to die will live (Luke 17:33). God wants us to see that there is a life that is contrary to this life.

The Spirit of the Lord reveals the following to us in the Word of God: *"He who believes in the Son has everlasting life; and he who does not believe the Son shall not see life"* (John 3:36). The unbelieving person is living and walking about but not seeing life. There is a life that is always brought into condemnation, which is living in death. There is a life that is free from condemnation—living in the Life.

Interpretation of Tongues

God the Author, the Finisher, the bringing into, the expression in the human life, changing it from that downward grade and lifting it and bringing it into a place of revelation to see that God has designed me to be greater than anything in the world.

I want you all to understand today that the design of God's Son for us is to be so much greater in this world than we have ever comprehended. God's design is not for me to stay where I was when I came into this room. God's plan is that the spiritual revelation will bring me into touch with a divine harmony. God wants me to touch ideals today; He wants me to reach something more. My eyes are looking up; my heart is looking up. My heart is big and enlarged in the presence of God, for I want to hear one word from God: "Come up higher." God will give us that—the privilege of going higher into a holy association.

There is a word of helpfulness in the first verse of Romans 8: *"There is therefore now no condemnation."*

This is the most important thing in all the world; there is nothing to be compared to it. It is beyond all you can think. The person who is under no condemnation has the heavens opened above him. This person has the smile of God upon him. This person has come into the realm of faith and joy and knows that his prayers are answered. I know that He hears me when I pray—I know I have the petition.

So God the Holy Spirit would have us to understand that there is a place in the Holy Spirit where there is no condemnation. This place is holiness, purity, righteousness, higher ground, perfection, and being more perfected in the presence of God. This higher ground state is holy desire. It is perfection where God is bringing us to live in such a way that He may smile through us and act upon us until our bodies become a flame of light ignited by Omnipotence. This is God's plan for us in the inheritance. It is an inheritance in the race that God wants us in today. This race, this divine race, this crowned race, this divine place is for us today.

There is no condemnation. The great secret of the plan of God for those who are in it is to see our covering. Oh, the covering; oh, the enfolding; oh, those eyes, those lovely eyes, that lovely Jesus, that blessed assurance of being strengthened, that knowledge of the Rock of Ages cleft for me, that place where I know I am! And that joy unbounding where I know there are neither devils nor angels nor principalities nor powers to interfere with that life in Christ (Rom. 8:38–39)! It is wonderful!

"No weapon formed against you shall prosper" (Isa. 54:17). God makes us devil-proof, whether evil reports or good reports (2 Cor. 6:8) are spread about

us. The power of the Most High God has put us in Christ. If we had put ourselves in, it would have been different. We were in the world, but God took us out of the world and put us into Christ, so God today by His Spirit wants us to see how this regenerative power, this glorious principle of God's high thoughtfulness, is for us. God wants me to leave myself in His sweetness. Oh, there is a sweetness about the Lord; oh, there is a glorious power behind us when God is behind us; there is a wonderful going before when He goes before us. He said, "I will go before you, and I will be your rear guard." (See Isaiah 52:12.) And so I see that God the Holy Spirit wants me today to penetrate or bring forth or show forth the glorious joy there is in this wonderful incarnation of the Spirit for us all in Christ Jesus. Glory to God!

> It reaches me, it reaches me,
>> Wondrous grace it reaches me,
> Pure, exhaustless, ever flowing,
>> Wondrous grace it reaches me.

The Word Makes Us Free

I can see this order of life that God has for us now: it is to make me free from the law of sin and the law of death. Praise the Lord! And I find that all sin leads down; it is like gravity. But I find that all faith lifts up into a place of admiration of God. So God wants to spread forth His wings and show that He is able, He is the Almighty, and He is able to preserve what we have committed to Him, because He is our Lord. He is not only our Creator, but also the

Only Believe

One who preserves us. He has not only redeemed
me, but He is also preserving me. I see I cannot do
any of these things by myself, but He has made it
possible that if I believe, He will do it.

I absolutely believe that the Word I am preaching
to you is sent forth by the power of the Spirit. I find
that God has strengthened your hands and is preparing you for the race, the race that is set before you
(Heb. 12:1). It is the divine plan I want to ask for in
my life so that I may be absolutely in the place where
I am preserved from all evil. These are days when Satan seeks to be very great. Oh, yes, he is tremendously
busy seeking those whom he may devour (1 Pet. 5:8),
but I am finding out that God has blessed me and has
blessed us so that we will be in a place where we are
more than overcomers (Rom. 8:37).

Being more than overcomers is to have a shout at
the end of the fight. It not only means overcoming,
but it also means being able to stand when we have
overcome, and not fall down. I count it a great privilege that God has opened my eyes to see that His
great plan has been arranged for us before the foundation of the world, and we may all just come into line
with God to believe that these things that He has
promised must come to pass to whoever believes.

Turn back once more to the thought that no
man, whoever he is, will ever make progress unless
he learns that he is greater than the Adversary. If
you don't learn, if you don't understand, if you don't
come into line today with the thought that you are
greater than the Adversary, you will find out that
you have a struggle in your life. I want to breathe
through you today a passage that is in Scripture,
which is, *"He who is in you"* (1 John 4:4). I don't

175

want to take anybody out of his bearings; I want to be so simple that everyone who hears this truth will know that he has a fortification, that he has the oracles of God behind him. In truth he has the power of God with him to overcome Satan through the blood of the Lamb. *"Who is he who overcomes...but he who believes that Jesus is the* [Christ]?" (1 John 5:5), for it is he who overcomes the world, even through his faith (v. 4).

Now faith is the supreme, divine position where God is entrenched, not only in the life, but also through the life, the mind, and the body. You will never find that you are at all equal against the power of the enemy except on the authority that you have an authority laid down within you. He who believes in his heart is able to move the mountain (Mark 11:23), but you do not believe in your heart until your heart is made perfect in the presence of God. As you think in your heart, so you are. *"Blessed are the pure in heart, for they shall see God"* (Matt. 5:8). These are the people who see this truth that I am presenting to you today, and it is in them, and that makes them *"more than conquerors"* (Rom. 8:37). They have life over sin, life over death, life over diseases, life over the devil. Praise the Lord!

Interpretation of Tongues

God is not the Author of confusion but the Author of peace and brings to life and focuses the eye until it sees God only, and when you come there you will stand.

Oh, the thought, the standing, the pure hands, the clean hearts—God the Holy Spirit has designed this for us within the plan of this realm of grace. God's plan is hidden, lost, completely lost to the devil, who is not able to come near. God covers; He hides; we are sealed; bless the Lord! We are sealed until the day of redemption. We so believe in the authority of the Almighty that we triumph in this glorious realm. Oh, this divine touch of God to the human soul brings us all to say all things are possible.

> Praise the Lord 'tis so, praise the Lord 'tis so,
>   Once I was blind but now I see,
> Once I was bound but now I am free,
>   Through faith I have the victory,
> Praise the Lord 'tis so.

And so the Lord has a great plan for us today to see, or rather to bring us to our wealth in Christ. Our wealth is so rich, beyond all comparison. *"Deep calls unto deep"* (Ps. 42:7). The Lord has prepared for us not only a sonship, but also an heirship, not only an heirship, but also a joint-heirship. We are not only feeling the breath of God, but the breath of God is also moving us. We are not only touching fire, but fire is also burning everything that cannot stand fire. And so in this holy sea of life, this divine inheritance for us, I see the truth so full of joy unspeakable today, and I see it and I read it to you. *"There is therefore now no condemnation to those who are in Christ Jesus"* (Rom. 8:1). Oh, hallelujah!

The Law of Life

Then I notice clearly that we must see and we must always get the facts of these truths. It is a law.

Well, there is a law of gravity, and there is a law of life, and we must see the difference and live in life that ceases to die. On the other hand, we must live a life that continues to die and to die daily, because when we die, we receive life. In that life, the baptism of the Holy Spirit is a baptism into a death, into a likeness unto death, into the Son of Man in His likeness. The baptism of the Holy Spirit is purifying, energizing, and it brings the soul to where it touches ideal immensity. God wants us to have no other plan in our mind but this.

Now come along with me, for the Lord has many things to say to us. I see that the devil wants to destroy. Now listen, you will find that John 10:10 is more real than ever. It says that the devil comes to steal because he is a thief, and then if he can steal, he will destroy: he will kill, and then he will destroy. I also find that Jesus comes along with a flood tide of refreshment and says, "I have come with life, with life and abundance of life." Abundance of life means that you live in an activity of divine inspiration, that you never touch the other thing. You are above it. You are only in association with it to pray it through or to cause the salt to be saltier or the light to be brighter until others can see the way. It is a foundation of God's principle, and everyone who knows it says that is God.

I will go a little further to help you. I find out that whatever you learn from me—I say it without fear of any contradiction—God has given you another chance of seeing light and life. If you fail to seize the opportunity, you will find you will be worse tomorrow. God speaks through me to tens of thousands all over. God is sending me forth to stir the people to diligence. Mine is not an ordinary message. You will never find I have an ordinary message. The past tense is an ordinary message. I must be on fire. The day is too late for me to stop; I must be catching fire; I must be in the wing. I am intensely in earnest and mean all I say now.

Within are the thoughts to impregnate you today with a desire from heaven, to let you see that you do not have to give place to the devil, neither in thought nor in word. And I pray to God the Holy Spirit that you will be so stirred that you will have a conviction come over your soul that you dare not disbelieve any of the truth, but rather the whole body will be aflame with the epistle of truth. *"He who has seen Me has seen the Father"* (John 14:9). Is that so? Oh, He said, "I and my Father will come and dwell in you." (See verse 23.) Yes, and when He comes to dwell in us, it is to be the epistle, it is to be the manifestation, the power; it is to be the Son of God working miracles, destroying the power of the devils, casting out evil spirits, and laying hands on the people so they who were dying under the power of the devil will live.

This is life divine, and this is God's thought for you now, if you will not fail to recognize the good hand of God coming to us, God speaking to us of these deep things of Himself that mean so much for us. Oh, bless God that I am entrusted with such a Gospel, with such a message, but first it burns in me.

You cannot bring anything to anybody else before you have reached it first yourself. You cannot talk beyond your wisdom. God brings you to test these things; then, because you desire to handle and because you chance to eat these things, out of the eating and digesting of these things will come the refining fire and the flood tide upon the dry ground. This is so because we will be a flame of fire for God: divine inspiration, catching the vision all the time and walking in the Holy Spirit. Oh, bless the Lord!

> I know the Lord, I know the Lord,
> I know the Lord has laid His hands on me.

Glory to Jesus! Is that good hand of God on me only? No! No! No! God has come to more than me, but the important thing is that we recognize the hand of God and the voice of God and that we recognize the power of God. We need to recognize how to be careful and gentle and how to have wisdom to abide in the anointing and to keep in the place where God is not only consuming fire, but also purifying fire. Glory to God! Oh, for this holy, intense zeal. Oh, that God would give us today this zealous position, which will absolutely put us in a place where we know this day that God has spoken to us. We know that once more this day God has brought before us another opportunity. This day—thank God that in His grace and kindness He has opened the way, beloved. The Lord speaks once, even more so, twice. God unfolds the kingdom to you, but He expects you to jump in and go through.

Swept Up in Faith

"There is therefore now no condemnation" (Rom. 8:1). I would not trade this truth for the money in a million banks. What does it mean? There is condemnation that comes to us if we know that we ought to

be further on in the race than we are. Something has stopped us.

Freedom from condemnation means so much to me. I know I was baptized with the Holy Spirit. The Holy Spirit was not the life; Jesus is the life, but the Holy Spirit came to reveal the life. The Holy Spirit is not truth; Jesus is the truth, but the Holy Spirit is the Spirit of that truth. So I must see that God has so much for me today. I notice that to be without condemnation I must be in the just place with God.

It is a wonderful thing to be justified by faith, but I find there is a greater place of justification than this. I find this: because Abraham believed God, He accounted it to him as righteousness (Rom. 4:3). That was more than the other. God accounted it to him as righteousness because Abraham believed God. He imputed no sin, and therefore He gave him wings. When He imputed no sin, He lifted Abraham into the righteousness of God, lifted him out of himself into a place of rest, and God covered him there. Abraham has not received anything from the Lord that He is not willing to give to anyone now. I am seeing today that whatever I have reached, I am only on the rippling of the wave of the surface of God's intense zeal of love and compassion. He is always saying nothing less than this: "Come on." So I am going forward.

I am here with a whole heart to say, "Come with me," for the Lord has spoken good concerning His people, and He will give them the land of promise. *"No good thing will He withhold"* (Ps. 84:11). So I know that God is in the place to bless today, but I want you to catch the fire. I want you to come out of all your natural propensities, for I tell you nothing is as detrimental to your spiritual rising as your natural mind and your body. Nothing will destroy your spiritual life but your own self. Paul knew that, and therefore he said, "I count myself as rubbish." (See Philippians 3:8.)

Is there anything else? Yes! Paul said, *"I did not immediately confer with flesh and blood"* (Gal. 1:16). He was getting very near this truth. I tell you there are a good many natural associations. As a Jew he came over to the plan of redemption, where everything was absolute foolishness and rank hypocrisy in Jewish estimation.

Is there anything else? Certainly! "If I can only win Him." (See Philippians 3:8.) Oh, what understanding there was in Paul, what beautiful character! What God had revealed to him about this Nazarene King was worthy to make him come into line to see. I can understand today that God breathed upon Paul absolutely. It is the breath of divine order; it is the breath of desire. God breathes on, and as He breathed on him I see this.

Oh, to know! To know that so many years ago, God baptized me, and I can say without a shadow of a doubt that God has swept me on. You know it! How I have always longed to go. I tell you, if you come there, you will have to say "no" to a thousand things in your natural order, for your own hearts will deceive you. Be careful of your friends and relatives; they are always a damp rag or a wet blanket. God wants us to lean on Him and go on with Him and dare to believe Him. There is no condemnation (Rom. 8:1). Oh, how sweet the thought! Never mind, I am not here to crush or to bruise anyone. I am here in the Holy Spirit order I know: to make you long to come on, long to obey, long to say to everything that is not the high order of holiness, "Regardless of who misses the right path, I will go through."

> I'm going through, Jesus, I'm going through,
> I'll pay the price whatever others do,
> I'll take the way of the Lord's despised few,
> I'm going through, Jesus, I'm going through.

It is worth it all, praise the Lord, worth it all. Thank God, quickened by the Spirit, I have covered over forty-four thousand miles. You cannot comprehend it with your mind; it is too vast. At all places God in His Spirit has been moving me. I have seen the glory of God moving. I have had the pleasure of seeing two thousand people in the morning and over five thousand in the evening to hear me preach. What opportunities! What times of refreshment! What wonderful things one sees, and I realize that nothing from the past would do. You cannot rely upon anything in the past, and so I am realizing the truth now. It is this: I see it is a whole burnt offering; I see it is an offering in righteousness; I see it is an offering that is accepted; and I see it is a daily offering.

No past sanctification is good enough for today, and I find that this life leads you on to see that it is sanctification with an inward desire of being more perfected every day. While I know I was wonderfully saved, I find that it is being saved that moves me toward perfection. While I see salvation has designs within it for the coming of the King, I see it enriches me with a ceaseless warmth so that I cannot get out of it. Nothing will do unless I am absolutely heated up with this life, because I must see the King.

Since it came, Pentecost has been spoken against, and if there is not someone rising up against you, if there is not a war on, you are doing a bad job. I tell you this in sincerity, if you are not making the people mad or glad, there is something amiss with your ministry. If you leave people as you found them, God is not speaking through you. So, there must be an intensity of enlargement of this divine personality, of God in the soul, so absolutely bringing you to a place where you know it would be awful to remain two days in the same place. I do not know how it sounds, but I tell you, it is intense zeal.

Come on a little nearer now. There are opportunities. God has the right-of-way to the heart and life to bring them to a place where opportunities are made for the possibility of being accomplished. I am realizing that God must impress upon your heart around you, wherever you are, that He has an opportunity for you today. It will stand right in front of you, and by that means you will be brought into a place where you will convince the people because God is there. Without the shadow of a doubt, the Word of God is effective and destroying, and it brings about perfect life.

Clothed in Faith

I am going to close with one Scripture passage, because of the importance of it. I want to give you one more word of life. Turn with me to the fifth chapter of 2 Corinthians—it will have something to do with this important treasure. I see that if I preach anything less than these things, I find I miss the whole opportunity of my life. I must have a ministry of faith; I must have clothing for this ministry of faith; I must have the Spirit of Life to manifest this ministry of faith; and then I must have the convincing evidence through the power of the Spirit of imparting that to the lives of the people. I pray that you will lay hold of this truth.

We have here in this fifth chapter one of the best things that God has given me now for some time, this ministry of life. *"For we who are in this tent groan, being burdened, not because we want to be unclothed, but further clothed, that mortality may be swallowed up by life"* (v. 4). Here is one of the greatest truths that was in this Pentecostal evidence, or life in evidence, or the evidence in the life. I find that Jesus is not coming to fetch the body—that is perfectly in order, we cannot get away from the fact— but Jesus is coming for the life in the body. The body may die, but that body will not be in the glory. God will give us a body, and the only thing He is going to give is life. The life is not your life, but it is His life in you. He who dwells in God has God dwelling in him (1 John 4:16). Jesus came to give us His life. Paul says, "Now I live, yet not I, but He lives His life." (See Galatians 2:20.) We read in Colossians 3:4 that when He who is our life appears, then we will appear.

You will find that you do not have a desire outside the desire of pleasing Him. There is a joy, or fullness of expression of all the joy, where you see His life being manifested in your mortal body, and that makes you so free from the natural life. Then you are joined up to the supernatural. Paul said he wanted to go, not to be unclothed but clothed upon (2 Cor. 5:4). There is a thought. Do we want to go? No! No! That is not the order of the body; that is not the order of the natural man; that is not the order of the human. What does he want? He wants to be so clothed upon; that is the first thing, clothed upon. When? Now!

Is there anything else? Yes! It is the life clothed upon and the life within the body eating up every mortality, every sense, every human desire, everything that has caused grief, sorrow, brokenness of heart, and has interfered with our rest, stopping the shining of our faces, making us feel how sorry we are. God wants to have His way with us, live in us to eat up everything, until the body will only be a body filled with the Spirit life. Then the body will only be an existence as the temple for the Spirit. But the body will be preserved blameless. The body, the soul, the spirit in the world will be blameless, and the coming of the King will take the life and change it to present it with Him. God will bring us there.

As sure as I have had this fellowship with you in the Spirit, as sure as your heart has been warmed, I say to you: never mind the past. You may have a thousand things that spoil you; forget them. Know that God has overcome for you so that you will overcome and will be presented faultless, even more so, spotless in the presence of the King. This life will eat up mortality—hallelujah!

The law of the life of the Spirit of Christ will make you free from the law of sin and death (Rom. 8:2). Can I attain this today? This is a problem; "I have failed a thousand times," you say. Never mind. Is your heart warmed? Do you want to be conquered, or do you love to come into line with Him? Will you pay the price for it? What is the desire of your heart? You may be sorry for the past, but let God have you for the future. You would not like to remain as you were before you came here. I know you would not; you exactly feel the position. You say, "Lord, forgive everything of the past, but help me, Lord, today to offer an offering in righteousness before you. Today I give myself afresh."

18

By Faith

We read in the Word that by faith Abel offered unto God a more excellent sacrifice than Cain (Heb. 11:4). We also read that by faith Enoch was taken away so that he would not see death (v. 5); by faith Noah prepared an ark to the saving of his household (v. 7); by faith Abraham, when he was called to go out into the place that he would receive for an inheritance, obeyed (v. 8).

There is only one way to all the treasures of God, and that is the way of faith. All things are possible, even the fulfilling of all promises is possible, to him who believes (Mark 9:23). And it is all by grace; *"by grace you have been saved through faith, and that not of yourselves; it is the gift of God"* (Eph. 2:8).

There will be failure in our lives if we do not build on the base, the Rock Christ Jesus. He is the only way. He is the truth. He is the life. Moreover, the Word He gives us is life-giving. As we receive the Word of Life, it quickens, it opens, it fills us, it moves us, it changes us, and it brings us into a place where we dare to say amen to all that God has said.

Beloved, there is a lot in an amen. You never get any place until you have the amen inside of you. That was the difference between Zacharias and Mary. When the Word came to Zacharias, he was filled with unbelief until the angel said, *"You will be mute...because you did not believe my words"* (Luke 1:20). Mary said, *"Let it be to me according to your word"* (v. 38). And the Lord was pleased that she believed that there would be a performance of what He had spoken. When we believe what God has said, there will be a performance.

Belief Becomes Fact

Let's look at the twelfth chapter of Acts, and we will find that there were people waiting all night and praying that Peter might come out of prison. But there seemed to be one thing missing despite all their praying, and that was faith. Rhoda had more faith than all the rest of them. When the knock came at the door, she ran to it, for she was expecting an answer to her prayers. The moment she heard Peter's voice, she ran back and announced to them that Peter was standing at the door. And all the people said, "You are mad. It isn't so." That was not faith. When she insisted that he was there, they said, "Well, perhaps God has sent his angel." (See verses 14–15.) But Rhoda insisted, "It is Peter." And Peter continued knocking. They went out and found it so (v. 16). What Rhoda had believed had become a glorious fact.

Beloved, we may do much praying and groaning, but we do not receive from God because of that; we receive because we believe. Still, sometimes it takes

God a long time to bring us through the groaning and the crying before we can believe.

I know that no man by his praying can change God, for you cannot change Him. Finney said, "Can a man who is full of sin and all kinds of ruin in his life change God when he starts to pray?" No, it is impossible. But when a man labors in prayer, he groans and travails because his tremendous sin is weighing him down, and he becomes broken in the presence of God. When properly melted, he comes into perfect harmony with the divine plan of God, and then God can work in that clay. He could not before. Prayer changes hearts, but it never changes God. He is the same yesterday, and today, and forever: full of love, full of compassion, full of mercy, full of grace, and ready to bestow this and communicate that to us as we come to Him in faith.

Believe that when you come into the presence of God you can have all you came for. You can take it away, and you can use it, for all the power of God is at your disposal in response to your faith. The price for all was paid by the blood of Jesus Christ at Calvary. Oh, He is the living God, the One who has power to change us! *"It is He who has made us, and not we ourselves"* (Ps. 100:3). And it is He who purposes to transform us so that the greatness of His power may work through us. Oh, beloved, God delights in us, and when a man's ways please the Lord, then He makes all things move according to His own blessed purpose.

Communion with God

We read in Hebrews 11:5, *"By faith Enoch was taken away so that he did not see death...before he was taken he had this testimony, that he pleased God."* I believe it is in the mind of God to prepare us for being taken away. But remember this, being taken away comes only on the line of holy obedience and a walk according to the good pleasure of God.

We are called to walk together with God through the Spirit. It is delightful to know that we can talk with God and hold communion with Him. Through this wonderful baptism in the Spirit that the Lord gives us, He enables us to talk to Him in a language that the Spirit has given, a language that no man understands but that He understands, a language of love. Oh, how wonderful it is to speak to Him in the Spirit, to let the Spirit lift and lift and lift us until He takes us into the very presence of God! I pray that God by His Spirit may move all of us so that we walk with God as Enoch walked with Him. But beloved, it is a walk by faith and not by sight, a walk of believing the Word of God.

I believe there are two kinds of faith. All people are born with a natural faith, but God calls us to a supernatural faith that is a gift from Himself. In the twenty-sixth chapter of Acts, Paul tells us of his call, how God spoke to him and told him to go to the Gentiles:

> *To open their eyes, in order to turn them from darkness to light, and from the power of Satan to God, that they may receive forgiveness of sins and an inheritance among those who are sanctified by faith in Me.* (Acts 26:18)

The faith that was in Christ was to be given by the Holy Spirit to those who believed. From this

point on, as Paul yielded his life to God, he could
say,

> *I have been crucified with Christ; it is no longer
> I who live, but Christ lives in me; and the life
> which I now live in the flesh I live by faith in
> the Son of God, who loved me and gave Himself
> for me.* (Gal. 2:20)

The faith of the Son of God is communicated by the
Spirit to the one who puts his trust in God and in
His Son.

Understand God's Word

I believe that all our failures come because of
an imperfect understanding of God's Word. I see
that it is impossible to please God on any other line
except by faith, and everything that is not of faith is
sin (Rom. 14:23). You say, "How can I obtain this
faith?" You see the secret in Hebrews 12:2: *"Looking unto Jesus, the author and finisher of our
faith."* He is the Author of faith. Oh, the might of
our Christ, who created the universe and upholds it
all by the might of His power! God has chosen Him
and ordained Him and clothed Him, and He who
made this vast universe will make us a new creation. He spoke the Word, and the stars came into
being; can He not speak the Word that will produce
a mighty faith in us? This One who is the Author
and Finisher of our faith comes and dwells within
us, quickens us by His Spirit, and molds us by His
will. He comes to live His life of faith within us and
to be to us all that we need. And He who has begun

a good work within us will complete it and perfect it (Phil. 1:6), for He is not only the Author but also the Finisher and Perfecter of our faith (Heb. 12:2).

For the word of God is living and powerful, and sharper than any two-edged sword, piercing even to the division of soul and spirit, and of joints and marrow, and is a discerner of the thoughts and intents of the heart. (Heb. 4:12)

How the Word of God severs the soul and the spirit—the soul that has a lot of carnality, a lot of selfishness in it, a lot of evil in it! Thank God, the Lord can sever from us all that is earthly and sensual and make us a spiritual people. He can bring all our selfishness to the place of death and bring the life of Jesus into our being to take the place of that earthly and sensual thing that is destroyed by the living Word.

The Word of God comes in to separate us from everything that is not of God. It destroys. It also gives life. He must bring to death all that is carnal in us. It was after the death of Christ that God raised Him up on high, and as we are dead with Him, we are raised up and made to sit in heavenly places in the new life that the Spirit gives.

God has come to lead us out of ourselves into Himself and to take us from the ordinary into the extraordinary, from the human into the divine, and to make us after the image of His Son. Oh, what a Savior! What an ideal Savior! It is written,

Beloved, now we are children of God; and it has not yet been revealed what we shall be, but we

know that when He is revealed, we shall be like Him, for we shall see Him as He is.

(1 John 3:2)

Even now, the Lord wants to transform us from glory to glory, by the Spirit of the living God. Have faith in God, have faith in the Son, have faith in the Holy Spirit; and the triune God will work in you to will and to do all the good pleasure of His will (Phil. 2:13).

19

Like Precious Faith

e are so dull of comprehension because we so often let the cares of this world blind our eyes, but if we can be open to God we will see that He has a greater plan for us in the future than we have ever seen or dreamed of in the past. It is God's delight to make possible to us what seems impossible, and when we reach a place where He alone has the right-of-way, then all the things that have been misty and misunderstood are cleared up.

God's Gift to Us

Let's look at 2 Peter 1:1–8:

To those who have obtained like precious faith with us by the righteousness of our God and Savior Jesus Christ: Grace and peace be multiplied to you in the knowledge of God and of Jesus our Lord, as His divine power has given to us all things that pertain to life and godliness, through the knowledge of Him who called us by glory and virtue, by which have been given to us exceedingly great and precious promises, that through these you may be partakers of the divine nature, having escaped the corruption that is in the world through lust. But also for this very reason, giving all diligence, add to your faith virtue, to virtue knowledge, to knowledge self-control, to self-control perseverance, to perseverance godliness, to godliness brotherly kindness, and to brotherly kindness love. For if these things are yours and abound, you will be neither barren nor unfruitful in the knowledge of our Lord Jesus Christ. (2 Peter 1:1–8)

This *"like precious faith"* that Peter was writing about is a gift that God is willing to give to all of us, and I believe God wants us to receive it so that we may subdue kingdoms, work righteousness, and, if the time has come, to stop the mouths of lions (Heb. 11:33). Under all circumstances we should be able to triumph, not because we have confidence in ourselves, but because our confidence is only in God. It is always those people who are full of faith who have a good report, who never murmur, who are in the place of victory, who are not in the place of human order but of divine order, since God has come to dwell in them.

The Lord Jesus is the Divine Author and brings into our minds the "Thus says the Lord" every time. We cannot have anything in our lives, except when we have a "Thus says the Lord" for it. We must see to it that the Word of God is always the standard of everything.

This *"like precious faith"* is for us all. But there may be some hindrance in your life that God will have to deal with. At one point in my life, it seemed as if I had had so much pressure come over my life to break me up like a potter's vessel. There is no other way into the deep things of God except by a broken spirit. There is no other way into the power of God. God will do for us exceedingly abundantly above all we ask or think (Eph. 3:20) when He can bring us to the place where we can say with Paul, "I live no longer" (see Galatians 2:20), and Another, even Christ, has taken the reins and the rule.

We are no better than our faith. Whatever your estimation is of your ability, or your righteousness, you are no better than your faith. No one is ever any better than his faith. He who believes that Jesus is the Son of God overcomes the world (1 John 5:5). How? This Jesus, upon whom your faith is placed— the power of His name, His personality, His life, His righteousness—are all made yours through faith. As you believe in Him and set your hope only on Him, you are purified even as He is pure. You are strengthened because He in whom you trust is strong. You are made whole because He who is all your confidence is whole. You may receive of His fullness, all the untold fullness of Christ, as your faith rests wholly in Him.

I understand God by His Word. I cannot understand God by impressions or feelings. I cannot get to know God by sentiments. If I am going to know God, I am going to know Him by His Word. I know I will be in heaven, but I cannot determine from my feelings that I am going to heaven. I am going to heaven because God's Word says it, and I believe God's Word. And *"faith comes by hearing, and hearing by the word of God"* (Rom. 10:17).

God's Real Working

There is one thing that can hinder our faith: a conscience that is seared. Paul sought to have a conscience void of offense (Acts 24:16). There is a conscience that is seared, and there is a conscience that is so opened to the presence of God that the smallest thing in the world will drive it to God. What we need is a conscience that is so opened to God that not one thing can come into and stay in our lives to break up our fellowship with God and shatter our faith in Him. And when we can come into the presence of God with clear consciences and genuine faith, our hearts not condemning us, then we have confidence toward God (1 John 3:21), *"and whatever we ask we receive from Him"* (v. 22).

In Mark 11:24 we read, *"Therefore I say to you, whatever things you ask when you pray, believe that you receive them, and you will have them."* Verse twenty-three speaks of mountains removed and difficulties cleared away. Sugarcoating won't do. We must have reality, the real working of our God. We must know God. We must be able to go in and converse with God. We must also know the mind of God toward us, so that all our petitions are always on the line of His will.

As this *"like precious faith"* becomes a part of you, it will make you so that you will dare to do anything. And remember, God wants daring men: men who will dare all, men who will be strong in Him and dare to do exploits. How will we reach this place of faith? Give up your own mind. Let go of your own thoughts, and take the thoughts of God, the Word of God. If you build yourself on imaginations, you will go wrong. You have the Word of God, and it is enough.

A man gave this remarkable testimony concerning the Word: "Never compare this Book with other books. Comparisons are dangerous. Never think or say that this Book contains the Word of God. It is the Word of God. It is supernatural in origin, eternal in duration, inexpressible in value, infinite in scope, regenerative in power, infallible in authority, universal in interest, personal in application, inspired in totality. Read it through. Write it down. Pray it in. Work it out. And then pass it on."

And truly the Word of God changes a man until he becomes an epistle of God. It transforms his mind, changes his character, moves him on from grace to grace, makes him an inheritor of the very nature of God. God comes in, dwells in, walks in, talks through, and dines with him who opens his being to the Word of God and receives the Spirit who inspired it.

When I was going over to New Zealand and Australia, there were many there to see me off. An Indian doctor rode in the same car with me to the docks and boarded the same ship. He was very quiet and took in all the things that were said on the ship. I began to preach, of course, and the Lord began to work among the people. In the second class of the ship, there was a young man and his wife who were attendants for a lady and gentleman in the first class. And as these two young people heard me talking to them privately and otherwise, they were very much impressed. Then the lady they were attending got very sick. In her sickness and her loneliness, she could find no relief. They called in the doctor, and the doctor gave her no hope.

And then, when in this strange dilemma—she was a great Christian Scientist, a preacher of it, and had gone many places preaching it—they thought of me. Knowing the conditions, and what she lived for, knowing that it was late in the day, that in the condition of her mind she could only receive the simplest word, I said to her, "Now you are very sick, and I won't talk to you about anything except this: I will pray for you in the name of Jesus, and the moment I pray you will be healed."

And the moment I prayed she was healed. That was this *"like precious faith"* in operation. Then she was disturbed. I showed her the terrible state she was in and pointed out to her all her folly and the fallacy of her position. I showed her that there was nothing in Christian Science, that it is a lie from the beginning and one of the last agencies of hell. At best it is a lie: preaching a lie and producing a lie.

Then she came to her senses. She became so penitent and brokenhearted. But the thing that stirred her first was that she had to go preach the simple gospel of Christ where she had preached Christian Science. She asked me if she had to give up certain things. I won't mention the things; they are too vile. I said, "No, what you have to do is to see Jesus and take Jesus." When she saw the Lord in His purity, the other things had to go. At the presence of Jesus, all else goes.

This opened the door. I had to preach to all on the boat. This gave me a great chance. As I preached, the power of God fell, conviction came, and sinners were saved. They followed me into my cabin one after another. God was working there.

Then this Indian doctor came. He said, "What will I do? Your preaching has changed me, but I must have a foundation. Will you spend some time with me?"

"Of course I will."

Then we went alone, and God broke the fallow ground. This Indian doctor was going right back to his Indian conditions under a new order. He had left a practice there. He told me of the great practice he had. He was going back to his practice to preach Jesus.

If you have lost your hunger for God, if you do not have a cry for more of God, you are missing the plan. A cry must come up from us that cannot be satisfied with anything but God. He wants to give us the vision of the prize ahead that is something higher than we have ever attained. If you ever stop at any point, pick up at the place where you have left off, and begin again under the refining light and power of heaven. God will meet you. And while He will bring you to a consciousness of your own frailty and to a brokenness of spirit, your faith will lay hold of Him and all the divine resources. His light and compassion will be manifested through you, and He will send the rain.

Should we not dedicate ourselves afresh to God? Some say, "I dedicated myself last night to God." Every new revelation brings a new decision. Let us seek Him.

Smith Wigglesworth on Healing
Smith Wigglesworth

Meet a bride who is dying of appendicitis, a young man who has been lame for eighteen years, a betrayed husband who is on his way to kill his wife, and a woman who is completely deaf. Through Smith Wigglesworth's words and ministry, you will discover what happened in their lives and what can take place in your own life. Find out how you can personally receive God's healing touch and how God can use you to bring healing to others, just as He did through Smith Wigglesworth.

ISBN: 978-0-88368-426-9 • Trade • 208 pages

WHITAKER
HOUSE

Smith Wigglesworth on Heaven
Smith Wigglesworth

Illustrating his insights with many dramatic, real-life
examples, Smith Wigglesworth has a dynamic message
in store for those who are looking toward the Second
Coming. He explains how to prepare for your future in
eternity with God while experiencing the power and joy
of the Holy Spirit in the present. Discover God's plans
for you in this life and what He has in store for you in
heaven. You can know victorious living—
now and for all eternity.

ISBN: 978-0-88368-954-7 • Trade • 224 pages

WHITAKER
HOUSE

Greater Works:
Experiencing God's Power
Smith Wigglesworth

Smith Wigglesworth was extraordinarily used by God to see souls saved, bodies healed, and lives changed. Even in the face of death, he did not waver in his faith because he trusted the Great Physician. Your heart will be stirred as you read in Wigglesworth's own words the dramatic accounts of miraculous healings of people whom the doctors had given up as hopeless. Discover how God can enable you, too, to reach out to a hurting world and touch all who come your way with His love.

ISBN: 978-0-88368-584-6 • Trade • 576 pages

WHITAKER
HOUSE

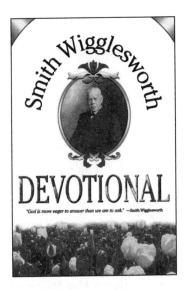

"God is more eager to answer than we are to ask." —Smith Wigglesworth

Smith Wigglesworth Devotional
Smith Wigglesworth

You are invited to journey with Smith Wigglesworth on a year-long trip that will quench your spiritual thirst while it radically transforms your faith. As you daily explore these challenging insights from the Apostle of Faith, you will connect with God's glorious power, cast out doubt, and see impossibilities turn into realities. Your prayer life will never be the same again when you personally experience the joy of seeing awesome, powerful results as you extend God's healing grace to others.

ISBN: 978-0-88368-574-7 • Trade • 560 pages

WHITAKER
HOUSE

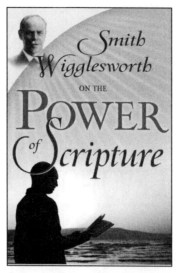

Smith Wigglesworth on the Power of Scripture
compiled by Roberts Liardon

Smith Wigglesworth knew the Bible thoroughly because it was the only book he ever read, and for years, the "Apostle of Faith" exhibited the power of Scripture to millions of believers in his legendary, miracle-filled meetings. Now, many of his teachings have been collected in one book, offering you the rare opportunity to sit at the feet of this anointed man of God. Transcribed exactly as they were delivered to a select group of Bible students, these teachings will allow you to develop your spiritual discernment, claim victory over temptation, and live in the freedom of God's grace. If you are ready to receive a fresh understanding of God's gifts and a fresh anointing of His power, you will cherish this glimpse into the heart and mind of one of His most gifted servants.

ISBN: 978-1-60374-094-4 • Trade • 384 pages

WHITAKER
HOUSE